DEBBIE MUMM'S
COUNTRY SETTINGS

STEP INTO THESE WARM AND INVITING SETTINGS

CREATED BY THIS GATHERING OF

DELIGHTFUL QUILTS

DEBBIE MUMM

DEAR FRIENDS,

Welcome to *Debbie Mumm's® Country Settings*.

This book is a dream come true for me. I always enjoy offering new quilts and other projects, but I've been wanting to combine the quilts with some of my other products to create beautiful room vignettes, so I'm very excited to share these settings we've created with you.

I love working with themes. When I design fabrics, quilts, dinnerware, and other home products, my goal is for them to complement each other. When planning the book, my creative team and I visualized different types of rooms and themes that would showcase the dinnerware and accessory pieces and show you how fun and easy it is to decorate your home with them.

Each chapter focuses on a favorite home setting ~ from vintage country kitchens to lovely garden patios ~ and in each you'll find many new ideas for decorating your home with charming wall quilts, cheery table quilts, colorful tablerunners, placemats, cozy lap quilts, plus much more.

One of my favorite settings was "Breakfast In Bed." That's probably because my guest room was the location for this vignette, and I always love an excuse to redecorate! The tea nook was also photographed in my dining room.

One of the very special features of this book is my artwork which we've used to decorate its pages. It was so fun choosing from my favorite images to complement the projects and dinnerware. I think this playful feature will add to your enjoyment of the book.

So fluff your pillows, pour a cup of soothing tea, and settle back to enjoy browsing through *Country Settings*. I'm sure you'll find ideas for warm and inviting country decorating on each inspiring page.

♥ *Debbie Mumm*

Special thanks go to those who generously opened their homes to our camera crews to be photographed for our book. Each of them helped us create the vision of *Country Settings!*

Thanks to Patti Eaton and her shop, Hawthorne Gallery, in Dayton, Washington. Her lovely home and delightful collectibles from her shop were used in our *"Country Vintage Kitchen."*

Hawthorne Gallery
245 E. Main Street
Dayton, Washington 99328
Toll Free (888) 882-3137

Thanks also to Carisa Dami for use of the garden porch (faux painting by Debbie's friend Lynn Guier) at her new Victorian home high in the hills north of Spokane for our *"Garden Party"* setting.

1116 E. Westview Ct., Spokane, WA 99218
(509) 466-3572 • Fax (509) 466-6919

Toll Free (888) 819-2923
www.debbiemumm.com

TABLE ☼ OF CONTENTS

CONTENTS

TEA TIME NOOK

Take a few moments out of your busy day to rest and reflect with a cup of warm tea. It's a well-deserved treat just for you. There's just something inviting about a cup of tea ... especially in your own delightful tea time nook. Set your table with a lovely quilt topped with your favorite tea set ... the personal touches that will make your tea party a special occasion.

TEAPOTS DINNERWARE

TEA TIME NOOK

5

TEA FOR SIX

WALLHANGING

Finished Size: 29" square

Photo: page 4

DECLARE YOUR FONDNESS FOR TEA

with this charming, colorful wallhanging. Bold letters spell it out for all to see while delicate teacups await your pleasure. You'll be delighted with the quick-pieced construction. Why not celebrate with a rainy-day party for five of your closest quilting friends? Read all instructions before beginning and use ¼"-wide seams throughout.

Quilt Layout

FABRIC REQUIREMENTS

Directional fabrics are not recommended.

Fabric A *(cups, saucers, and handles)*
   10" square each of six fabrics

Fabric B *(background)* - ¾ yard

Fabric C *(letters)* - ¼ yard

Accent Border - ⅙ yard

Border - ⅜ yard

Backing - 1 yard

Binding - ⅜ yard

Lightweight batting - 33" square

CUTTING THE STRIPS AND PIECES

Pre-wash and press fabrics. Using rotary cutter, see-through ruler, and cutting mat, cut the following strips and pieces. If indicated, some will need to be cut again into smaller strips and pieces. The approximate width of the fabric is 42".

Measurements for all pieces include ¼"-wide seam allowance.

Fabric A

From each 10" square, cut

* One 5½" square *(teacups)*

* One 1½" x 5½" rectangle *(saucers)*

Fabric B *(background)*

* Four 1½" x 21½" strips

* One 1½" x 22½" strip

* Two 2½" x 42" strips, cut into
  • Seven 2½" x 6½" pieces
  • Two 2½" x 5½" pieces
  • Two 2½" x 3½" pieces
  • One 2½" x 1½" piece

* Two 1½" x 42" strips, cut into
  • Four 1½" x 6½" pieces
  • One 1½" x 4½" piece
  • One 1½" x 3½" piece
  • Twenty-six 1½" squares

Fabric C *(letters)*

* Two 1½" x 42" strips, cut into
  • Three 1½" x 6½" pieces
  • Two 1½" x 5½" pieces
  • One 1½" x 4½" piece
  • One 1½" x 3½" piece
  • Two 1½" x 2½" pieces
  • Twelve 1½" squares

* One 2½" x 5½" piece

Accent Border

* Four 1" x 42" strips

Border

* Four 3" x 42" strips

Backing

* One 33" square

Binding

* Four 2¾" x 42" strips

MAKING THE BLOCKS

You'll be making six Teacup Blocks and three alphabet blocks, one each for the letters "T," "E," and "A."

Whenever possible, use the assembly line method for each step. Position pieces with right sides together and line up next to your sewing machine. Stitch the first unit together then continue sewing others without breaking threads. When all units are sewn, clip threads to separate them. Press in direction of arrows in diagrams.

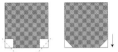

TEACUP BLOCKS

For all blocks, refer to Quick Corner Triangle directions on page 110. Block will measure 6½" x 7½".

1. **Cup Unit:** Sew a 1½" Fabric B square to two adjacent corners of a 5½" Fabric A square. Press. Make a total of six.

A = 5½ x 5½
B = 1½ x 1½
Make 6

2. **Saucer Unit:** Sew a 1½" Fabric B square to each end of a 1½" x 5½" Fabric A rectangle. Press. Make a total of six.

A = 1½ x 5½
B = 1½ x 1½
Make 6

3. Sew a cup unit from step 1 to a contrasting-color saucer unit from step 2. Press toward saucer. Make a total of six.

Make 6

CREATE YOUR OWN CENTERPIECE

Who says a teapot is just for serving tea? With a few added touches, it can be magically transformed into a charming centerpiece for your tea table.

For a look at the delightful teapots designed by Debbie Mumm®, see the color photo on page 4. Once you've picked just the right one, the next step is to add your personal touch to it.

How about filling it with delightful flowers from your garden … bright yellow daffodils in the spring or sunny zinnias in the summer. If your garden isn't in bloom, try filling your teapot with a pot of ivy-the perfect finishing touch to your tea party.

4. Refer to Hand Appliqué directions on page 110. Trace cup handle from pattern on page 10, using Fabric A scraps. Position a contrasting color handle for each teacup and appliqué to 2½" x 6½" Fabric B piece, referring to project layout on page 6 for placement.

5. Sew unit from step 4 to right side of each cup-and-saucer unit. Press. Make a total of six.

Make 6

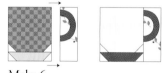 ALPHABET BLOCKS

LETTER "T":

1. Sew two 1½" Fabric C squares to opposite corners of each 2½" x 5½" Fabric B piece. Press. Make one of each following diagrams.

B = 2½ x 5½
C = 1½ x 1½
Make 1 of each

2. Sew 2½" x 5½" Fabric C piece between units from step 1. Press.

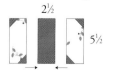

2½

5½

3. Sew one 1½" x 6½" Fabric C piece and one 1½" x 6½" Fabric B piece to unit from step 2. Press. Block will measure 6½" x 7½".

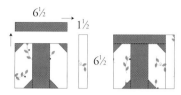

6½

1½

6½

LETTER "E":

1. Sew a 1½" Fabric C square to each end of a 1½" x 6½" Fabric B piece. Press.

B = 1½ x 6½
C = 1½ x 1½

2. Repeat step 1 to sew a 1½" Fabric C square to each end of 1½" x 4½" Fabric B piece. Press.

B = 1½ x 4½
C = 1½ x 1½

3. Sew the 1½" x 3½" Fabric C piece between the 1½" x 3½" Fabric B piece and one 2½" x 3½" Fabric B piece. Press.

3½

1½

1½

2½

4. Sew unit from step 3 between 1½" x 4½" Fabric C piece and unit from step 2. Press.

1½

4½

5. Sew unit from step 4 between two 1½" x 5½" Fabric C pieces. Press.

6. Sew unit from step 5 between one 1½" x 6½" Fabric B piece and the unit from step 1. Press. Block will measure 6½" x 7½".

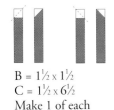

LETTER "A":

1. Sew a 1½" Fabric B square to one end of remaining 1½" x 6½" Fabric C pieces. Make one each following diagrams. Press.

B = 1½ x 1½
C = 1½ x 6½
Make 1 of each

2. Repeat step 1 to sew one 1½" Fabric C square to a 2½" x 6½" Fabric B piece and to remaining 1½" x 6½" Fabric B piece. Press.

B = 2½ x 6½
    1½ x 6½
C = 1½ x 1½
Make 1 of each

3. Sew a 1½" Fabric C square to adjacent corners of a remaining 2½" x 3½" Fabric B piece. Press.

B = 2½ x 3½
C = 1½ x 1½

4. Sew 2½" x 1½" Fabric B piece between two 2½" x 1½" Fabric C pieces. Press.

2½
1½
1½
1½

5. Arrange and sew units from steps 1– 4 as shown. Press. Block will measure 6½" x 7½".

ASSEMBLY

1. Referring to project layout on page 6, arrange one horizontal row of alphabet blocks (to spell TEA) and two horizontal rows of three Teacup Blocks. Sew blocks into rows. Press.

2. Arrange and sew together 1½" x 21½" Fabric B strips, Teacup rows, and Alphabet row as shown. Press.

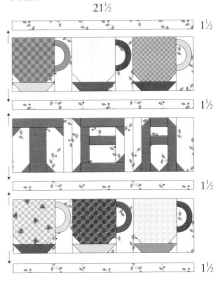

21½
1½
1½
1½
1½

3. Sew 1½" x 22½" Fabric B strip to left side of unit. Press.

BORDERS

1. Measure quilt through center from side to side. Trim two 1" x 42" accent border strips to this measurement. Sew to top and bottom of quilt top. Press toward accent border.

2. Measure quilt through center from top to bottom, including accent border. Trim remaining 1" x 42" accent border strips to this measurement. Sew to sides. Press.

3. Repeat measuring as described in step 1. Cut two 3" x 42" border strips to this measurement and sew to top and bottom. Press toward outside border.

4. Repeat measuring as described in step 2. Cut remaining 3" x 42" border strips to this measurement. Sew to sides. Press.

LAYERING AND FINISHING

1. Arrange and baste backing, batting, and top together, referring to Layering the Quilt directions on page 111.

2. Hand or machine quilt as desired.

3. Refer to Binding the Quilt directions on page 111, and use 2¾" x 42" strips for binding.

A NOTE FROM DEBBIE . . .

*Sharing our hearts
and a cup of tea
With friends is always a
special time.*

*Why not call a friend
and plan
To have tea this very week!
Whether at home or in your
favorite tearoom,
make some time
and make some memories
together.*

Love, Debbie

*from the book
Tea Time Friends
Brownlow©1999
illustrated by Debbie Mumm®*

cup handle
trace 6

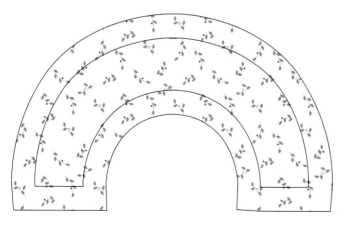

TEAPOTS DINNERWARE

This festive dinnerware invites friends and family to the table for an afternoon of warm scones and tea. For information on where to buy Debbie Mumm® dinnerware, visit www.debbiemumm.com or call (888) 819-2923.

BUTTER CUP

TABLE QUILT

Finished Size: 65" square

Photo: page 11

BREEZY BUTTERCUPS,

LATTICE-LIKE SASHING,

a maze of crisp, crisscrossing garden paths. No matter the season, it feels like summer when this cheerful quilt graces your table. Read all instructions before beginning and use ¼"-wide seams throughout.

Quilt Layout

FABRIC REQUIREMENTS

Directional fabrics are
not recommended.

Fabric A *(buttercups)* - ⅓ yard each
of six different fabrics

Fabric B *(buttercup backgrounds)*
⅓ yard each of four different
fabrics

Fabric C *(buttercup centers)*
Twenty-four 1½" squares from
assorted scraps

Fabric D *(corner, chain, and partial
chain blocks)* - ¼ yard each of
four different fabrics

Fabric E *(chain background)*
1¾ yards

Inside Accent Borders - ⅙ yard each
of three different fabrics

Sashing - ⅞ yard

Outside Accent Border - ¼ yard

Border - ¾ yard

Binding - ⅔ yard

Backing - 4 yards

Lightweight batting - 69" square

INSTRUCTIONS

CUTTING THE STRIPS AND PIECES

Read first paragraph of Cutting the Strips and Pieces on page 7.

Fabric A *(buttercups)*

* Two 3½" x 42" strips, cut into
  * Sixteen 3½" x 2½" pieces
  * Eight 3½" x 1½" pieces
* One 1½" x 42" strip, cut into
  * Eight 1½" squares

Repeat for each of six fabrics.

Fabric B *(buttercup backgrounds)*

* Two 2½" x 42" strips, cut into
  * Twenty-four 2½" squares
* Two 1½" x 42" strips, cut into
  * Forty-eight 1½" squares

Repeat for each of four fabrics.

Fabric D *(corner squares, chain, and partial chain blocks)*

* Three 1½" x 27" strips
* One 1½" x 6" piece, cut into
  * Three 1½" squares

Repeat for each of four fabrics.

Fabric E *(chain background)*

* Two 6½" x 42" strips, cut into
  * Twelve 6½" squares
* Two 3½" x 42" strips, cut into
  * Twelve 3½" x 6½" pieces

* Two 4½" x 27" strips
* Six 2½" x 27" strips
* Four 1½" x 27" strips
* One 1½" x 42" strip, cut into
  * Eight 1½" x 2½" pieces
  * Eight 1½" squares

Inside Accent Borders

* Four 1" x 42" strips

Repeat for each of three fabrics.

Sashing

* Six 1½" x 42" strips
* Nine 1½" x 42" strips, cut into
  * Four 1½" x 39½" strips
  * Twenty-four 1½" x 7½" pieces

Outside Accent Border

* Six 1" x 42" strips

Border

* Seven 3½" x 42" strips

Binding

* Eight 2¾" x 42" strips

MAKING THE BLOCKS

You will be making twenty-four Buttercup Blocks, four Corner Blocks, thirteen Chain Blocks, and eight Partial Chain Blocks. Each Buttercup Block pairs a single Fabric A and Fabric B and has a scrappy Fabric C center. The block will measure 7½" square. The Corner, Chain, and Partial Chain Blocks combine a variety of medium fabrics (Fabric D) with a consistent light background (Fabric E).

The size of the Corner Block is 3½" square; the Chain Block, 6½" square; and the Partial Chain Block, 6½" x 3½".

Whenever possible, use the assembly line method for each step. Position pieces right sides together and line up next to your sewing machine. Stitch first unit together, then continue sewing others without breaking threads. When all units are sewn, clip threads to separate them. Press in direction of arrows in diagrams.

TEA·TIME·NOOK

13

BUTTERCUP BLOCKS

For all blocks, refer to Quick Corner Triangle directions on page 110.

1. For each block, sew one 1½" Fabric C square between two matching 1½" Fabric A squares. Press. Make a total of twenty-four.

1½
□ ■ □ 1½
Make 24

2. Sew unit from step 1 between two matching 3½" x 1½" Fabric A pieces. Press. Make a total of twenty-four.

3½
□ 1½
■
□
Make 24

3. Refer to Quick Corner Triangle directions on page 110. For each block, sew two matching 1½" Fabric B squares to each of four matching 3½" x 2½" Fabric A pieces. Press. Make a total of ninety-six.

A = 3½ x 2½
B = 1½ x 1½
Make 96

4. For each block, sew unit from step 3 between two matching 2½" Fabric B squares. Press. Make a total of forty-eight.

2½
2½
Make 48

5. Sew unit from step 2 between two matching units from step 3. Press. Make a total of twenty-four.

Make 24

6. For each block, sew unit from step 5 between two matching units from step 4. Press. Make a total of twenty-four. Block will measure 7½" square.

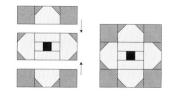

CORNER BLOCKS

1. Sew one 1½" Fabric D square between two 1½" Fabric E squares. Press. Make a total of four.

1½
□ ■ □ 1½
Make 4

2. Sew one 1½" Fabric D square to one 1½" x 2½" Fabric E piece. Press. Make a total of eight.

2½ 1½
□ ■ 1½
Make 8

3. Sew unit from step 1 between two units from step 2. Press. Make a total of four. Block will measure 3½" square.

Make 4

 CHAIN AND PARTIAL CHAIN BLOCKS

1. Sew two different 1½" x 27" Fabric D strips together lengthwise. Sew one 2½" x 27" Fabric E strip to each side as shown. Repeat to make two strip sets. Press. Using rotary cutter and ruler, cut seventeen 1½" segments from each strip set for a total of thirty-four segments.

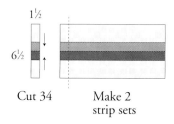

1½

6½

Cut 34   Make 2 strip sets

2. Sew one 2½" x 27" Fabric E strip between two different 1½" x 27" Fabric D strips and two 1½" x 27" Fabric E strips. Repeat to make two strip sets. Press. Cut seventeen 1½" segments from each strip set for a total of thirty-four segments.

1½

6½

Cut 34   Make 2 strip sets

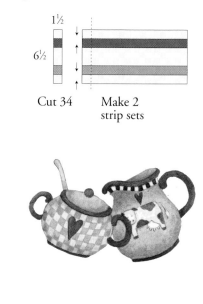

3. Sew one 4½" x 27" Fabric E strip between two different 1½" x 27" Fabric D strips. Repeat to make two strip sets. Press. Cut a total of seventeen 1½" segments from each strip set for a total of thirty-four segments.

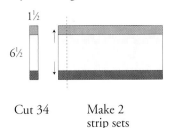

Cut 34   Make 2 strip sets

4. For each Chain Block, sew two different units from step 1 between two units each from steps 2 and 3 as shown. Press. Make a total of thirteen. Block will measure 6½" square.

Make 13

5. For each Partial Chain Block, sew one unit from step 2 between one unit from step 1 and one unit from step 3. Press. Make a total of eight. Block will measure 6½" x 3½".

Make 8

ASSEMBLY

1. Arrange two Corner Blocks, two Partial Chain Blocks, and three 3½" x 6½" Fabric E pieces in a horizontal row as shown. Sew and press. Make two rows.

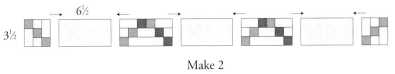

Make 2

2. Arrange three Chain Blocks, two 3½" x 6½" Fabric E pieces, and two 6½" Fabric E squares in a horizontal row. Sew and press. Make three rows.

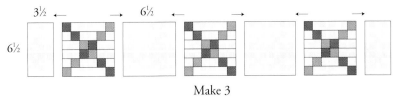

Make 3

3. Arrange two Chain Blocks, three 6½" Fabric E squares, and two Partial Chain Blocks in a horizontal row. Sew and press. Make two rows.

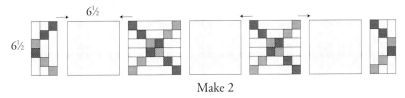

Make 2

4. Referring to project layout on page 12, arrange rows in correct order. Join rows and press. Center unit will measure 36½" square.

🫖 BORDERS

1. Measure quilt through center from side to side. Trim two matching 1" x 42" inside accent border strips to this measurement. Sew to top and bottom. Press toward accent border.

2. Measure quilt through center from top to bottom, including border. Trim remaining matching 1" x 42" inside accent border strips to this measurement. Sew to sides. Press.

3. Repeat steps 1 and 2 to add second set of matching top, bottom, and side inside accent border strips to quilt. Press.

4. Repeat steps 1 and 2 to add third set of matching top, bottom, and side inside accent border strips to quilt. Press.

5. Lay out a pleasing arrangement of five Buttercup Blocks alternating with four 1½" x 7½" sashing strips. Sew and press. Make two rows.

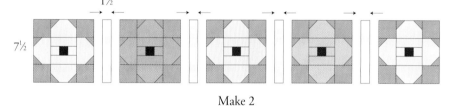

Make 2

6. Sew 1½" x 39½" sashing strips to top and bottom edges of pieced rows from step 5. Press toward sashing strips.

7. Sew sashed rows from step 6 to top and bottom of quilt. Press toward sashed rows.

8. Lay out a pleasing arrangement of seven Buttercup Blocks alternating with eight 1½" x 7½" sashing strips. Sew and press. Make two rows.

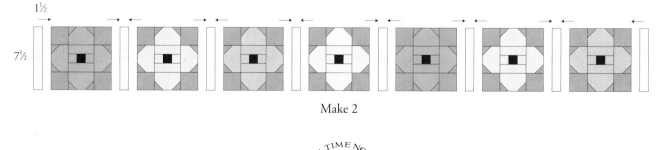

Make 2

9. Sew remaining 1½" x 42" sashing strips together to make one continuous 1½"-wide strip. From this strip, cut four 1½" x 57½" sashing strips. Sew sashing strips to top and bottom edges of pieced rows from step 8. Press toward sashing strips.

10. Sew sashed rows from step 9 to sides of quilt. Press toward sashed rows.

11. Sew 1" x 42" outside accent border strips together to make one continuous 1"-wide strip. Measure and cut two outside accent border strips as in step 1. Sew to top and bottom. Press toward sashing strips.

12. Measure and cut two 1"-wide outside accent border strips as in step 2. Sew to sides. Press.

13. Sew 3½" x 42" border strips together to make one continuous 3½"-wide strip. Repeat steps 11 and 12 to fit, trim, and sew 3½"-wide border strips to top, bottom, and sides of quilt. Press toward border.

LAYERING AND FINISHING

1. Cut backing fabric crosswise into two equal pieces. Sew pieces together to make one 72" x 84" (approximate) backing piece. Arrange and baste backing, batting, and top together referring to Layering the Quilt directions on page 111.

2. Hand or machine quilt as desired.

3. Sew 2¾" x 42" binding strips together in pairs. Refer to Binding the Quilt directions on page 111 to finish.

FOR A PERFECT ACCENT . . .

. . . create tea napkins to coordinate with your Buttercup Table Quilt. Choose a luscious shade of yellow to match the array of buttercups on the quilt, or choose a color that is a perfect complement to your own tea time nook. They are a quick and easy project that will give that special personal touch to your tea table.

For each napkin you will need:

• One 12½" square of fabric (napkin)

• One 13½" square of fabric (napkin)

• Two 1" x 12½" strips (contrasting trim)

• Two 1" x 13 ½" strips (contrasting trim)

To make the napkin:

• Sew the two 1" x 12½" strips on the top and bottom of the 12½" square. Press toward napkin. Sew the 1" x 13½" strips to the sides. Press.

• Position the unit from step 1 and the 13½" square with right sides together. Using a ¼" inch seam, sew around all four sides, leaving a 2" opening on one side for turning.

• Turn right side out and press.

• Hand stitch side opening closed.

• Repeat for each napkin.

SUNFLOWER STARS QUILT

Finished Size: 43" square

Photo: page 4

WHETHER DRAPED

OVER A TABLE,

cupboard, or buffet, this sunny topper
adds special-occasion sparkle to even
the most casual family mealtime.
Star-inspired sunflowers dance
around a large center panel–
the perfect showcase for a favorite
fabric. Read all instructions
before beginning and use
¼"-wide seams throughout.

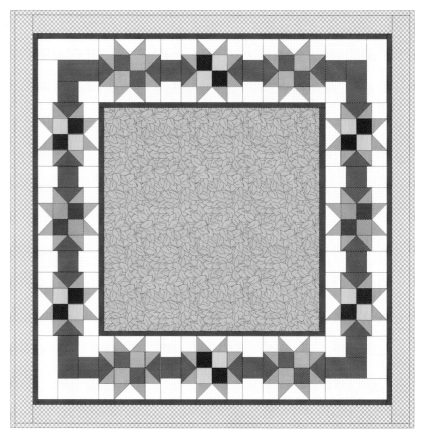

Quilt Layout

FABRIC REQUIREMENTS

Fabric A *(sunflower petals)* - ⅓ yard

Fabric B *(background)* - ⅔ yard

Fabric C *(vine spacer and vine corner blocks)* - ⅜ yard

Fabric D *(sunflower centers)*
One 2" x 10" strip each of twelve different fabrics

Center Square - ⅔ yard

Inside Accent Border - ¼ yard

Outside Accent Border - ¼ yard

Border - ⅓ yard

Binding - ½ yard

Backing - 2⅝ yard

Lightweight batting - 47" square

CUTTING THE STRIPS AND PIECES

Read first paragraph of Cutting the Strips and Pieces on page 7.

Fabric A *(sunflower petals)*

❋ Five 2" x 42" strips, cut into
  • Ninety-six 2" squares

Fabric B *(background)*

❋ Two 2½" x 42" strips *(vine spacer blocks)*

❋ Two 2½" x 42" strips, cut into
  • Four 2½" x 6½" pieces *(vine corner blocks)*
  • Four 2½" x 4½" pieces *(vine corner blocks)*
  • Four 2½" squares *(vine corner blocks)*

❋ Five 2" x 42" strips, cut into
  • Twenty-four 2" x 3½" pieces *(sunflower blocks)*
  • Forty-eight 2" squares *(sunflower blocks)*

Fabric C

❋ One 2½" x 42" strip *(vine spacer blocks)*

❋ One 2½" x 42" strip, cut into
  • Four 2½" x 4½" pieces *(vine corner blocks)*
  • Four 2½" squares *(vine corner blocks)*

❋ Three 2" x 42" strips, cut into
  • Twenty-four 2" x 3½" pieces *(sunflower blocks)*

Center Square

❋ One 22½" square

Inside Accent Border

❋ Two 1½" x 24½" strips
❋ Two 1½" x 22½" strips

Outside Accent Border

❋ Four 1½" x 42" strips

Border

❋ Four 2½" x 42" strips

Binding

❋ Five 2¾" x 42" strips

❋ *Delightful Debbie Mumm® teapots can be a colorful accent to your home with her wallpaper border from Imperial Home Décor Group. Call (800) 539-5399 or visit www.imp-wall.com.*

MAKING THE BLOCKS

You'll be making twelve Sunflower Blocks, eight Vine Spacer Blocks, and four Vine Corner Blocks.

Whenever possible, use the assembly-line method for each step. Position pieces with right sides together and line up next to your sewing machine. Stitch the first unit together, then continue sewing others without breaking threads. When all units are sewn, clip threads to separate them. Press in direction of arrows in diagrams.

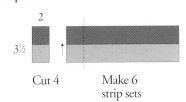

SUNFLOWER BLOCKS

1. Sew 2" x 10" Fabric D strips together in pairs to make six strip sets. Press seams toward darker fabrics. Using rotary cutter and ruler, cut four 2"-wide segments from each strip set.

2

3½

Cut 4   Make 6 strip sets

2. Sew matching segments together in pairs as shown to make twelve four-patch units. Press.

Make 12

3. Refer to Quick Corner Triangle directions on page 110. Sew one 2" Fabric A square to each 2" x 3½" Fabric B rectangle as shown. Press. Make a total of twenty-four.

A= 2 x 2
B= 2 x 3½
Make 24

4. Sew a second 2" Fabric A square to each unit from step 3. Press.

A/B = 2 x 3½
Make 24

5. Repeat steps 3 and 4 to sew two 2" Fabric A squares to each 2" x 3½" Fabric C rectangle. Press. Make a total of twenty-four.

Make 24

6. Sew one unit from step 4 between two 2" Fabric B squares. Press. Make a total of twenty-four.

Make 24

7. Sew one four-patch unit from step 2 between two units from step 5. Press. Make a total of twelve.

Make 12

8. Sew units from step 7 between two units from step 6 as shown. Press. Make a total of twelve. Block will measure 6½" square.

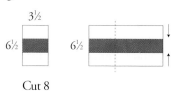

Make 12

🍵 VINE BLOCKS

1. For Vine Spacer Blocks, sew one 2½" x 42" Fabric C strip between two 2½" x 42" Fabric B strips to make a strip set. Press toward Fabric C. Cut eight 3½"-wide segments.

Cut 8

2. For Vine Corner Squares, sew 2½" Fabric B and 2½" Fabric C squares together in pairs. Make a total of four. Press.

Make 4

3. Sew 2½" x 4½" Fabric C rectangles to units from step 2. Make four. Press toward Fabric C rectangles.

Make 4

4. Sew 2½" x 4½" Fabric B rectangles to units from step 3. Make a total of four. Press toward step 3 unit.

Make 4

5. Sew 2½" x 6½" Fabric B rectangles to units from step 4. Make a total of four. Press.

Make 4

ASSEMBLY

1. Sew 1½" x 22½" inside accent border strips to top and bottom of 22½" center square. Press toward accent border. Sew 1½" x 24½" inside accent border strips to sides of center square. Press.

2. Arrange and sew together three Sunflower and two Vine Spacer Blocks to make four rows. Press seam allowances toward vine spacer blocks.

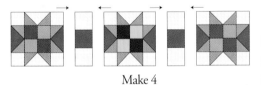

Make 4

3. Fit, pin, and sew one row each from step 2 to top and bottom of quilt. Press toward accent border.

4. Referring to quilt diagram on page 18, sew 6½" Vine Corner Squares to each end of remaining rows. Press toward corner squares. Fit, pin, and sew to sides. Press.

5. Measure quilt through center from side to side. Trim two 1½"-wide outside accent border strips to this measurement. Sew to top and bottom. Press toward accent border.

6. Measure quilt through center from top to bottom, including accent borders. Trim remaining 1½"-wide outside accent border strips to this measurement. Sew to sides. Press.

7. Sew 2½" x 42" border strips end to end to make one continuous 2½"-wide strip.

8. Repeat measuring as described in step 5. Cut two 2½"-wide strips to this measurement from border strip. Sew to top and bottom of quilt. Press seams toward outside border.

9. Repeat measuring as described in step 6. Cut two strips to this measurement from remaining 2½"-wide border strip. Sew to sides. Press.

LAYERING AND FINISHING

1. Cut backing fabric crosswise into two equal pieces. Sew pieces together to make one 47" x 84" (approximate) backing piece. Arrange and baste backing, batting, and top together, referring to Layering the Quilt directions on page 111.

2. Hand or machine quilt as desired.

3. Refer to Binding the Quilt directions on page 111, and use 2¾" x 42" strips to finish.

BREAKFAST IN BED

IMAGINE A LUXURIOUS *Sunday morning. The warm sun is spilling through your bedroom window, and you have all the time in the world to enjoy it. You are relaxing in your bed that is adorned with a sunshine-colored quilt and mountains of soft pillows.*

For an added treat, you have just been served a breakfast of fresh walnut scones and raspberry tea in your favorite fanciful teacup. What a perfect setting. Can a day that starts this way be anything less than wonderful?

SPRING BOUQUET DINNERWARE

BREAKFAST IN BED

23

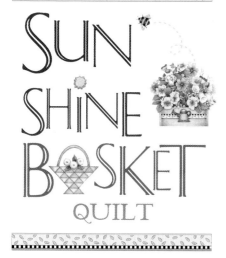

SUNSHINE BASKET QUILT

Finished Size: 49" square

Photo: page 31

WHAT COULD BE A MORE PERFECT

welcome for spring than a delicate pastel basket brimming with pretty posies? Graceful waving vines and a ring of sweet little baskets create a springtime mood. Tossed over the Basket Weave Quilt and coupled with a delightful pillow or two, this sunshine quilt dresses any bedtop in romantic style. Read all instructions before beginning and use ¼"-wide seams throughout.

Quilt Layout

FABRIC REQUIREMENTS

Fabric A (*background*) - 2 yards

Fabric B (*center basket block*) ⅝ yard

Fabric C (*center basket block*) ⅝ yard

Fabric D (*corner flower blocks*) ⅛ yard

Fabric E (*corner flower block centers*) Four 1½" squares

Fabric F (*small basket blocks*) ⅓ yard each of four different fabrics

First Accent Border - ⅛ yard

Appliqué Flowers - ⅛ yard or assorted scraps

Appliqué Flower Centers assorted scraps

Leaves - ⅛ yard or assorted scraps

Vines - ⅓ yard

Inside Setting Triangles One 8¾" square

Second Accent Border - ⅙ yard

Outside Setting Triangles - ⅝ yard

Third Accent Border - ¼ yard

Backing - 3 yards

Binding - ½ yard

Lightweight batting - 53" square

CUTTING THE STRIPS AND PIECES

Read first paragraph of Cutting the Strips and Pieces on page 7.

Fabric A (background)

* One 10⅞" square
* Four 4½" x 42" strips cut into
  • Twenty-eight 4½" squares
* Three 3½" x 42" strips, cut into
  • Eight 3½" x 12½" pieces
* Eleven 2½" x 42" strips, cut into
  • One 2½" x 14½" piece
  • Two 2½" x 10½" pieces
  • One 2½" x 8½" piece
  • One hundred fifty-three 2½" squares
* One 1½" x 42" strip, cut into
  • Sixteen 1½" squares

Fabric B (center flower basket)

* One 18" square, cut into
  • One 1" x 24" bias strip
* One 2½" x 22" strip, cut into
  • Eight 2½" squares

Fabric C (center flower basket)

* One 18" square, cut into
  • One 1" x 24" bias strip
* Two 4" squares
* Three 2½" squares

Fabric D (corner flower blocks)

* One 1½" x 42" strip, cut into
  • Eight 1½" x 3½" pieces
  • Eight 1½" squares

Fabric F (small basket blocks)

* One 4½" x 42" strip, cut into
  • Seven 4½" squares
* One 2½" x 42" strip, cut into
  • Fourteen 2½" squares

Repeat for each of four fabrics.

First Accent Border

* Two 1½" x 42" strips, cut into
  • Two 1½" x 16½" pieces
  • Two 1½" x 14½" pieces

Vines

* Two 10" squares, cut into
  • Eight 1" x 12" bias strips

Second Accent Border

* Four 1¼" x 42" strips

Outside Setting Triangles

* Two 18¼" squares

Third Accent Border

* Four 1½" x 42" strips

Binding

* Five 2¾" x 42" strips

DISPLAYING YOUR SUNSHINE QUILT

Our Sunshine Basket Quilt is a delightful topper for our Basket Weave Quilt shown on page 22.

Not only will it bring a touch of sunshine to your bedroom, it can also add whimsy and color to other spots in your home too. Try it in the middle of your dining room table, your sideboard, or your buffet. Its delicate appliquéd flowers and pieced baskets are sure to bring compliments from the guests at your next dinner party.

Or try it hanging on point in a special spot in your living room or entryway. It becomes an eye-catching wall quilt. Anywhere it's displayed, it will add just the right personal touch to your home.

MAKING THE BLOCKS

You will be making one Center Basket Block, four Corner Flower Blocks for the inside setting-triangle units, and twenty-eight Small Basket Blocks for the border.

Whenever possible, use the assembly line method for each step. Position pieces right sides together and line up next to your sewing machine. Stitch first unit together, then continue sewing others without breaking threads. When all units are sewn, clip threads to separate them. Press in direction of arrows in diagrams.

CENTER BASKET BLOCK

For all blocks, refer to Quick Corner Triangle directions on page 110.

1. Using 2½" Fabric A and Fabric B squares, make eight units. Press. Repeat, using 2½" Fabric A and Fabric C squares to make three units.

A = 2½ x 2½   A = 2½ x 2½
B = 2½ x 2½   C = 2½ x 2½
Make 8   Make 3

2. Cut each 4" Fabric C square twice diagonally to make eight triangles.

3. Arrange 2½" Fabric A squares, A/C and A/B units from step 1, and Fabric C quarter-square triangles into four rows as shown. Sew into rows. Press.

4. Join rows, carefully matching seams. Press. Add two Fabric C quarter-square triangles to finish unit as shown. Press.

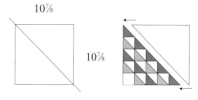

5. Cut 10⅞" Fabric A square in half once diagonally to make two triangles. Sew one triangle to unit from step 4. Press.

10⅞

10⅞

6. Sew one A/B unit from step 1 to 2½" x 8½" Fabric A piece. Press.

8½

2½

7. Sew unit from step 5 between unit from step 6 and one 2½" x 10½" Fabric A piece. Press.

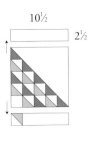

8. Sew remaining A/B unit between 2½" Fabric A square and 2½" x 10½" Fabric A piece. Press.

9. Sew unit from step 7 between 2½" x 14½" Fabric A piece and unit from step 8. Press. Block will measure 14½" square.

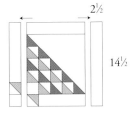

10. Sew 1½" x 14½" first accent border strips to opposite sides of block. Press seams toward accent border. Sew 1½" x 16½" first accent border strips to remaining two sides. Press.

FLOWER BASKET APPLIQUÉ

1. For basket handles, fold 1" x 24" Fabric B bias strip right sides together. Stitch along unfinished edge to make ¼" bias tube. Turn and press with ¼" bias bar. Repeat for 1" x 24" Fabric C bias strip.

2. Refer to Hand Appliqué directions on page 110. Position Fabric B and Fabric C bias strips side by side and machine baste across one pair of short raw edges to secure. Weave strips into a "braid" and stitch across raw edges to secure.

3. Refer to project layout on page 24 to position braided handle above basket with short raw edges overlapping seam. Machine or hand stitch handle in place, opening seams as necessary to insert raw edges of handle. Restitch seams. Press.

4. Refer to Hand Appliqué directions on page 110. Use appliqué patterns on page 30 to make templates for flower, flower center, and leaf. Trace six flowers on flower fabric, six flower centers on flower center fabric, and nine leaves on leaf fabric. Cut out appliqués, adding ¼" seam allowance around each piece.

5. Refer to project layout on page 24 to arrange flowers, flower centers, and leaves in basket. Appliqué in place.

CORNER FLOWER BLOCKS

1. Sew one 1½" Fabric E square between two 1½" Fabric D squares. Press. Make a total of four.

Make 4

2. Refer to Quick Corner Triangle directions on page 110. Sew two 1½" Fabric A squares to each 1½" x 3½" Fabric D piece. Press. Make a total of eight.

A = 1½ x 1½
D = 1½ x 3½
Make 8

3. Sew one unit from step 1 between two units from step 2. Press. Make a total of four. Block will measure 3½" square.

Make 4

CORNER TRIANGLES

1. Cut 8 ¾" square in half twice diagonally to make four inside setting triangles. Sew one 3½" x 12½" Fabric A strip to one short side of each triangle, aligning straight edges at corner. Press seams toward triangle.

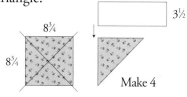

8¾
8¾
12½
3½
Make 4

2. Sew Corner Flower Blocks to one end of each remaining 3½" x 12½" Fabric A strip. Press seams toward Corner Blocks. Make a total of four.

3½
12½
Make 4

3. Sew units from step 2 to units from step 1 as shown, aligning straight edges at corners. Press seams toward triangles. Make a total of four.

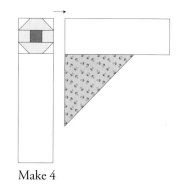

Make 4

4. Trim "tails" of Fabric A strips even with long raw edge of setting triangles.

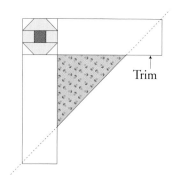

Trim

5. Sew one pieced corner triangle to each side of bordered center block. Press seams toward block accent border.

6. For vines, fold each 1" x 12" bias strip right sides together. Stitch along unfinished edge to make ¼" bias tube. Turn and press with ¼" bias bar. Make eight.

7. Refer to project layout on page 24. Position one ¼" x 12" bias vine on each Fabric A strip (two per corner), with vine's short raw edges overlapping seams. Machine or hand stitch vines in place, opening seams as necessary to insert raw edges of vine. Restitch seams. Press.

8. Refer to Hand Appliqué directions on page 110. Use leaf template to trace sixteen additional leaves on leaf fabric. Cut out appliqués, adding ¼" seam allowance around each piece.

9. Refer to project layout on page 24 to position two leaves along each appliquéd vine from step 7. Appliqué in place.

SMALL BASKET BLOCKS

1. Refer to Quick Corner Triangle directions on page 110. Using 2½" Fabric A and Fabric F squares, make fifty-six units. Press.

A = 2½ x 2½
F = 2½ x 2½
Make 56

2. For each basket base sew one 2½" Fabric A square to each unit from step 1 as shown. Make twenty-eight of each. Press.

2½
2½
Make 28 of each

3. Refer to Quick Corner Triangle directions on page 110. Using 4½" Fabric A and Fabric F squares, make twenty-eight units. Press.

A = 4½ x 4½
F = 4½ x 4½
Make 28

4. Sew one matching-colored unit from step 2 to bottom of unit from step 3. Press. Make a total of twenty-eight.

Make 28

5. Sew one 2½" Fabric A square to each remaining unit from step 2. Press. Make a total of twenty-eight.

2½
Make 28

6. Sew each unit from step 5 to matching-colored unit from step 4. Press. Block will measure 6½" square.

Make 28

7. From remaining scraps of Fabric F colors, cut seven 1" x 7" bias strips from each color. Fold each strip right sides together. Stitch along unfinished edge to make ¼" bias tube. Turn and press with ¼" bias bar. Make twenty-eight.

8. Position handles over matching-colored baskets with short raw edges overlapping seams as shown. Machine or hand stitch handles in place, opening seams as necessary to insert raw edges. Restitch seams. Press.

Open seam and insert raw edge

29

ASSEMBLY

1. Measure quilt through center from side to side. Trim two 1¼" x 42" second accent border strips to this measurement. Sew to top and bottom. Press seams toward accent border.

2. Measure quilt through center from top to bottom, including border. Trim remaining 1¼" x 42" second accent border strips to this measurement. Sew to sides. Press. At this point quilt will measure 24½" square.

3. Cut 18¼" squares in half once diagonally to make four outside setting triangles.

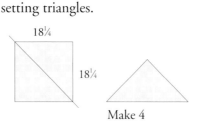

Make 4

4. Sew one corner triangle to each side of quilt. Press seams toward accent border.

5. Repeat steps 1 and 2 to fit, trim, and sew 1½"-wide border strips to top, bottom, and sides of quilt. Press seams toward border. Quilt will measure 36½" square.

6. Refer to project layout on page 24. Lay out a pleasing horizontal row of six small Basket Blocks and sew together. Press. Make a total of two rows.

7. Repeat step 6 to make two rows of eight small Basket Blocks. Press.

8. Sew rows from step 6 to opposite sides of quilt. Press seams toward accent strip. Sew rows from step 7

LAYERING AND FINISHING

1. Cut backing fabric crosswise into two equal pieces. Sew pieces together on the long edges to make one 54" x 84" (approximate) backing piece. Arrange and baste backing, batting, and top together referring to Layering the Quilt on page 111.

2. Hand or machine quilt as desired.

3. Cut one 2¾" x 42" binding strip into four equal pieces. Sew one piece to each remaining 2¾" x 42" strip. Refer to Binding the Quilt directions on page 111 to finish.

appliqué pattern pieces
Sunshine Basket Quilt

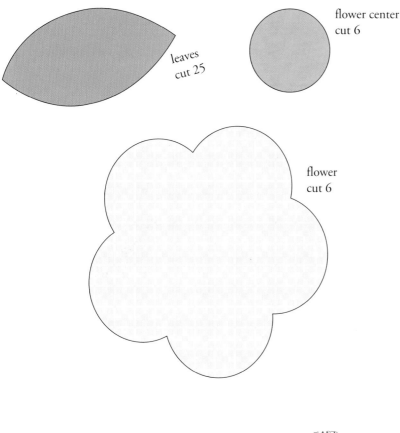

leaves
cut 25

flower center
cut 6

flower
cut 6

SPRING BOUQUET DINNERWARE

Treat yourself to breakfast in bed on this lovely pastel-colored dinnerware accented with bouquets of blooming flowers. For information on where to buy Debbie Mumm® dinnerware, visit www.debbiemumm.com or call (888) 819-2923.

BÄSKET

WEÄVE
QUILT

Finished Quilt Size: 91" x 100"

Photo: page 22

"HOW DID YOU

DO THAT?"

That's the question your friends will

ask as they admire the intricate basket

weave design of this clever quilt.

Only you will know how simple it

was with its quick and efficient

rotary-cut, strip-pieced construction.

Read all instructions before beginning

and use ¼"-wide seams throughout.

Quilt Layout

FABRIC REQUIREMENTS

Fabric A *(block 1 and block 3)*
1⅜ yards

Fabric B *(block 1 and block 3)*
1⅜ yards

Fabric C *(block 1 and block 3)*
1⅜ yards

Fabric D *(block 2 and block 3)*
1¼ yards

Fabric E *(block 2 and block 3)*
2¾ yards

Fabric F *(block 2 and block 3)*
1¼ yards

Backing - 8¼ yards

Binding - ⅞ yard

Lightweight batting
99" x 108" piece

FABRIC KEY

 Fabric A

Fabric B

Fabric C

Fabric D

Fabric E

 Fabric F

CUTTING THE STRIPS AND PIECES

Read first paragraph of Cutting the Strips and Pieces on page 7.

Fabric A strips *(block 1 and block 3)*
* Thirteen 3½" x 42" strips

Fabric B *(block 1 and block 3)*
* Thirteen 3½" x 42" strips

Fabric C *(block 1 and block 3)*
* Thirteen 3½" x 42" strips

Fabric D *(block 2 and block 3)*
* Twelve 3½" x 42" strips

Fabric E *(block 2 and block 3)*
* Twenty-seven 3½" x 42" strips

Fabric F *(block 2 and block 3)*
* Twelve 3½" x 42" strips

Binding
* Ten 2¾ " x 42" strips

MAKING THE BLOCKS

You will be making a total of one hundred ten blocks in three different block variations: thirty of block one, twenty-five of block two, and fifty-five of block three. All blocks will measure 9½" square.

Whenever possible, use the assembly line method for each step. Position pieces right sides together next to your sewing machine. Stitch first unit together, then continue sewing others without breaking threads. When all units are sewn, clip threads to separate them. Press in direction of arrows in diagrams.

BLOCK ONE

Sew one 3½" x 42" Fabric B strip between a 3½" x 42" Fabric A and Fabric C strip to make eight 9½" x 42" strip sets. Press. Using rotary cutter and ruler, cut thirty 9½" segments from strip sets. Label them Block One. Block will measure 9½" square.

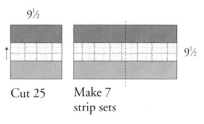

9½

Cut 30   Make 8
                strip sets

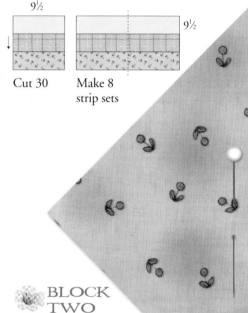

BLOCK TWO

Sew one 3½" x 42" Fabric E strip between a 3½" x 42" Fabric D and Fabric F strip to make seven 9½" x 42" strip sets. Press. Using rotary cutter and ruler, cut twenty-five 9½" segments from strip sets. Label them Block Two.

9½

Cut 25   Make 7
                strip sets

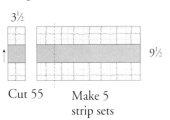

BLOCK THREE

1. Sew one 3½" x 42" Fabric A strip between two 3½" x 42" Fabric E strips to make five 9½" x 42" strip sets. Press. Using rotary cutter and ruler, cut fifty-five 3½" segments from strip sets.

3½

9½

Cut 55   Make 5
strip sets

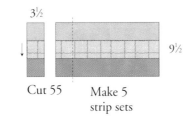

2. Sew one 3½" x 42" Fabric B strip between 3½" x 42" Fabric D and Fabric F strips to make five 9½" x 42" strip sets. Press. Using rotary cutter and ruler, cut fifty-five 3½" segments from strip sets.

3½

9½

Cut 55   Make 5
strip sets

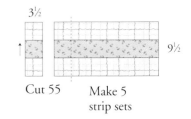

3. Sew one 3½" x 42" Fabric C strip between two 3½" x 42" Fabric E strips to make five 9½" x 42" strip sets. Press. Using rotary cutter and ruler, cut fifty-five 3½" segments from strip sets.

3½

9½

Cut 55   Make 5
strip sets

4. Sew one unit from step 2 between one unit from steps 1 and 3 as shown. Press. Make fifty-five. Label them Block Three. Block will measure 9½" square.

Make 55

MAKE IT SCRAPPY

Instead of the soft shades of pastels in the Basket Weave Quilt, how about creating it from dozens of bright prints, plaids and solids.

The quick and easy strip-piecing makes it perfect for using your collection of favorite fabrics. Try mixing up the most unlikely combinations of colors and prints ... the purple floral with the red and white checks or the homespun plaids with the elegant holiday print.

The result can be a lively quilt that will add a little whimsy wherever you use it.

ASSEMBLY

1. Arrange five Block One and five Block Three to make a horizontal row, alternating the two block variations as shown. Press seams toward Block One. Make six rows and label them Row A.

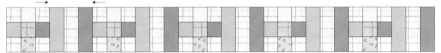

Make 6 rows
Row A

2. Arrange five Block Three and five Block Two in a horizontal row, alternating the two block variations as shown. Press seams toward Block Two. Make five rows and label them Row B.

Make 5 rows
Row B

3. Referring to layout on page 32, lay out alternating A and B rows. Begin with an A row. Join rows and press.

LAYERING AND FINISHING

1. Cut backing fabric crosswise into three equal pieces. Sew pieces together on long edges to make one 99" x 126" (approximate) backing piece. Arrange and baste backing, batting, and top together referring to Layering the Quilt directions on page 111.

2. Hand or machine quilt as desired.

3. Sew eight 2 ¾" x 42" binding strips together in pairs. Cut two remaining strips in half and sew halves to each pieced strip. Refer to Binding the Quilt directions on page 111 to finish.

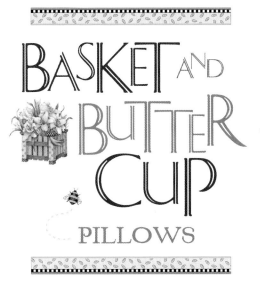

BASKET AND BUTTERCUP PILLOWS

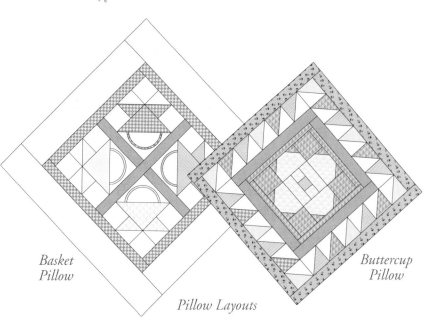

Basket Pillow

Buttercup Pillow

Pillow Layouts

Basket Pillow - 18" square

Buttercup Pillow - 16" square

Photo: page 22

THE PERFECT ACCENT TO OUR SUNSHINE

Basket Quilt, these cheery pillows are sure to brighten even the rainiest of mornings. Read all instructions before beginning and use ¼"-wide seams throughout.

FABRIC REQUIREMENTS

	Basket Pillow	Buttercup Pillow
Fabric A	⅙ yard each of four different fabrics *(baskets)*	¼ yard *(buttercup and border triangles)*
Fabric B	⅓ yard *(background)*	⅙ yard *(buttercup background and sashing)*
Fabric C		assorted scraps *(triangle border)*
Fabric D		assorted scraps *(triangle border)*
Sashing	⅛ yard	
Accent Border	⅛ yard *(accent)*	
Border	¼ yard	⅛ yard
Batting	22" square	20" square
Backing	½ yard	⅜ yard
Lining	22" square	20" square
Pillow Form	18"	16"

BASKET PILLOW

CUTTING THE STRIPS AND PIECES

Read first paragraph of Cutting the Strips and Pieces on page 7.

Fabric A *(baskets)*

* One 4½" square
* Two 2½" squares
* One 1" x 7" bias strip

Repeat for each of four fabrics.

Fabric B *(background)*

* One 4½" x 42" strip, cut into
  • Four 4½" squares
* Two 2½" x 42" strips, cut into
  • Twenty 2½" squares

Sashing

* One 1" x 42" strip, cut into
  • One 1" x 13" strip
  • Two 1" x 6½" strips

Accent Border

* Two 1" x 42" strips, cut into
  • Two 1" x 14" strips
  • Two 1" x 13" strips

Border

* Two 2¾" x 42" strips, cut into
  • Two 2¾" x 18½" strips
  • Two 2¾" x 14" strips

Backing

* One 12¾" x 42" strip, cut into
  • Two 12¾" x 18½" pieces

MAKING THE BLOCKS

BASKET BLOCKS

1. Refer to Small Basket Block directions on page 29. Repeat steps 1-8 for each of four Basket Blocks except-

* In step 1, make eight of each.
* In step 2, make four of each.
* In step 3, make four of each.
* In step 4, make four of each.
* In step 5, make four of each.
* In step 7, make four of each.

ASSEMBLY

1. Referring to project layout on page 36, arrange blocks to make two rows with two blocks each. Sew 1" x 6½" sashing strips between blocks. Press seams toward sashing strips. Sew 1" x 13" sashing strip between the two rows of blocks. Press.

2. Sew 1" x 13" accent border strips to top and bottom. Press seams toward accent border. Sew remaining accent border strips to sides. Press.

3. Sew 2¾" x 14" border strips to top and bottom and 2¾" x 18½" border strips to sides. Press seams toward border.

4. Layer batting between top and lining. Baste. Hand or machine quilt as desired. Trim batting and lining even with raw edge of pillow top.

LAYERING AND FINISHING

1. Narrow hem one long edge of each 12¾" x 18½" backing piece by folding under ¼" to wrong side. Press. Fold again ¼" to wrong side. Press. Topstitch along folded edge.

2. With right sides up, lay one backing piece over second piece so hemmed edges overlap, making single 18½" square backing panel. Baste pieces together at top and bottom where they overlap.

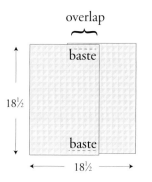

overlap

baste

18½

baste

18½

3. With right sides together, position and pin pillow top to backing. Using ¼" seam, sew around edges. Trim corners, turn right side out, and press.

4. Insert pillow form into pillow cover.

BUTTERCUP PILLOW

CUTTING THE STRIPS AND PIECES

Read first paragraph of Cutting the Strips and Pieces on page 7.

Fabric A

❋ Two 2½" x 42" strips, cut into

  • Four 2½" x 3½" pieces *(buttercup)*

  • Twenty-four 2½" squares *(border triangles)*

❋ One 1½" x 42" strip, cut into

  • Two 1½" x 3½" pieces *(buttercup)*

  • Two 1½" squares *(buttercup)*

Fabric B

❋ One 2½" x 14" strip, cut into

  • Four 2½" squares *(buttercup background)*

❋ One 1½" x 16" strip, cut into

  • Eight 1½" squares *(buttercup background)*

❋ One 1" x 42" strip, cut into

  • Two 1" x 8½" pieces *(sashing)*

  • Two 1" x 7½" pieces *(sashing)*

Fabric C

❋ One 1½" x 42" strip, cut into

  • One 1½" square *(buttercup center)*

  • Two 1½" x 10½" pieces *(accent border)*

  • Two 1½" x 8½" pieces *(accent border)*

Fabric D *(border triangles)*

❋ Twenty-four 2½" squares

Border

❋ Two 1½" x 42" strips, cut into

  • Two 1½" x 16½" strips

  • Two 1½" x 14½" strips

Backing

❋ One 11" x 42" strip, cut into

  • Two 11" x 16½" pieces

MAKING THE BLOCKS

BUTTERCUP BLOCK

1. Refer to Buttercup Block directions on page 14. Repeat steps 1-6 for one Buttercup Block except-

• In step 1, make one.

• In step 2, make one.

• In step 3, make four of each.

• In step 4, make two.

• In step 5, make one.

2. Sew 1" x 7½" sashing strips to top and bottom. Press seams toward sashing strips.

3. Sew 1" x 8½" sashing strips to sides. Press.

BORDERS

1. Sew 1½" x 8½" accent border strips to top and bottom. Press seams toward accent border. Sew 1½" x 10½" accent border strips to sides. Press.

2. Refer to Quick Corner Triangle directions on page 110. Using 2½" Fabric A and Fabric D squares, make twenty-four units. Press.

A = 2½ x 2½
D = 2½ x 2½
Make 24

3. Arrange five units from step 2 in a pleasing order. Sew together to make a strip. Press. Make four strips.

Make 4

4. Referring to project layout on page 36, sew a strip from step 3 each to top and bottom. Press seams toward accent border.

5. Sew one remaining unit from step 2 to each end of remaining strips from step 3 as shown. Sew to sides. Press.

6. Sew 1½" x 14½" border strips to top and bottom. Press seams toward border.

7. Sew 1½" x 16½" border strips to sides. Press.

8. Layer batting between top and lining. Baste. Hand or machine quilt as desired. Trim batting and lining even with raw edge of pillow top.

LAYERING AND FINISHING

1. Using two 11" x 16½" pieces for backing, refer to Layering and Finishing directions on page 38. Repeat steps 1-4, except, in step 2, overlap pieces making a single 16½" square backing panel.

GARDEN PARTY

HOW ABOUT A garden party? A blooming garden or a patio filled with pots of fragrant flowers can be the most festive spot in your home. Try having a picnic or a tea party among the blooms!

With all nature's colorful help, creating a perfect setting on your patio is easy. Add a table with your favorite tea set and Mother Nature will do the rest!

GARDEN VIGNETTE DINNERWARE

GARDEN PARTY

41

WELCOME SPRING QUILT

Finished Size: 57" x 75"

Photo: page 44

SPRING IS ALWAYS RIGHT AROUND THE

corner when you snuggle under this colorful little quilt, the perfect size for a decadent afternoon nap! Flowerlike shades of green and lavender combine to create a springtime mood. Read all instructions before beginning and use ¼"-wide seams throughout.

Quilt Layout

FABRIC REQUIREMENTS

Fabric A *(diamonds)* - ⅞ yard each of two different fabrics

Fabric B *(triangles)* - 1 yard each of green fabric and lavender fabric

Fabric C *(rectangles)* - ⅓ yard each of two different fabrics

Fabric D *(center squares)* - ⅛ yard each of two different fabrics

Lattice - 1½ yards

Corner Squares - ¼ yard

Accent Border - ¼ yard

Border - 1 yard

Binding - ⅝ yard

Backing - 3⅝ yards

Lightweight batting 65" x 82" piece

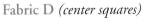

INSTRUCTIONS

CUTTING THE STRIPS AND PIECES

Read first paragraph of Cutting the Strips and Pieces on page 7.

Fabric A *(diamonds)*

* Seven 3½" x 42" strips, cut into
  * Seventy-two 3½" squares *(block one)*
* Six 3½" x 42" strips, cut into
  * Sixty-eight 3½" squares *(block two)*

Fabric B *(triangles)*

* Fifteen 2" x 42" strips, cut into
  * Two hundred eighty-eight 2" squares *(block one)*
* Fourteen 2" x 42" strips, cut into
  * Two hundred seventy-two 2" squares *(block two)*

Fabric C *(rectangles)*

* Seven 1½" x 42" strips, cut into
  * Seventy-two 1½" x 3½" pieces *(block one)*
* Six 1½" x 42" strips, cut into
  * Sixty-eight 1½" x 3½" pieces *(block two)*

Fabric D *(center squares)*

* One 1½" x 42" strip, cut into
  * Eighteen 1½" squares *(block one)*
* One 1½" x 42" strip, cut into
  * Seventeen 1½" squares *(block two)*

Lattice

* Seventeen 2½" x 42" strips, cut into
  * Eighty-two 2½" x 7½" pieces

Corner Squares

* Three 2½" x 42" strips, cut into
  * Forty-eight 2½" squares

Accent Border

* Six 1" x 42" strips

Border

* Seven 4½" x 42" strips

Binding

* Seven 2¾" x 42" strips

MAKING THE BLOCKS

You'll be making thirty-five blocks total: eighteen Block One (green triangles) and seventeen Block Two (lavender triangles).

Whenever possible, use the assembly line method for each step. Position pieces right sides together and line up next to sewing machine. Stitch first unit together, then continue sewing others without breaking threads. When all units are sewn, clip threads to separate them.

Press in the direction of the arrows in diagrams.

BLOCK ONE

1. Refer to Quick Corner Triangle directions on page 110. Sew four 2" Fabric B squares to each 3½" Fabric A square. Press. Make a total of seventy-two.

Step 1   Step 2

A = 3½ x 3½
B = 2 x 2
Make 72

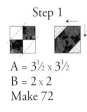

2. Sew one 1½" x 3½" Fabric C piece between two units from step 1. Press. Make a total of thirty-six.

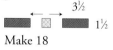

Make 36

3. Sew one 1½" Fabric D square between two matching 1½" x 3½" Fabric C pieces. Press. Make eighteen.

Make 18

4. Sew one unit from step 3 between two units from step 2. Press. Make eighteen. Block will measure 7½" square.

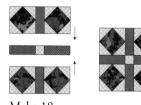

Make 18

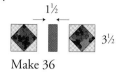 BLOCK TWO

1. Refer to Quick Corner Triangle directions on page 110. Sew four 2" Fabric B squares to each 3½" Fabric A square. Press. Make sixty-eight.

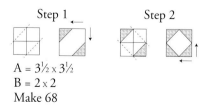

Step 1   Step 2

A = 3½ x 3½
B = 2 x 2
Make 68

2. Sew one 1½" x 3½" Fabric C piece between two units from step 1. Press. Make thirty-four.

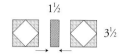

3. Sew one 1½" Fabric D square between two matching 1½" x 3½" Fabric C pieces. Press. Make seventeen.

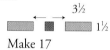

Make 17

4. Sew one unit from step 3 between two units from step 2. Press. Make seventeen. Block will measure 7½" square.

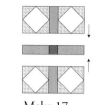

Make 17

LOVE IS NOT

ENOUGH

*Love of flowers
and vegetables
is not enough to make
a good gardener.
He must also hate weeds.*

Eugene P. Bertin

*from the book
How Does Your Garden Grow?
Brownlow©2000
illustrated by Debbie Mumm*

ASSEMBLY

1. Sew six 2½" corner squares and five 2½" x 7½" lattice pieces together in rows as shown. Repeat to make eight rows of lattice. Press.

2½ 7½

2½

Make 8

2. Refer to layout on page 42. Arrange blocks in seven horizontal rows with five blocks each, alternating Block One and Block Two in each row. Rows 1, 3, 5, and 7 begin with Block One, while Rows 2, 4, and 6 begin with Block Two.

3. For each row, sew 2½" x 7½" lattice pieces between blocks and to each end. Press seams toward lattice.

4. Sew lattice strips from step 1 to top and bottom and between rows of blocks. Press seams toward lattice.

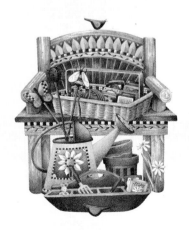

ADDING THE BORDERS

1. Sew 1" accent border strips end to end to make one 1"-wide strip. Measure quilt through center from side to side. Cut two 1"-wide accent border strips to this measurement. Sew to top and bottom. Press seams toward accent borders.

2. Measure quilt through center from top to bottom, including borders. Cut two 1"-wide accent border strips to this measurement. Sew to sides. Press.

3. Sew 4½" x 42" border strips to make one continuous 4½"-wide strip. Repeat steps 1 and 2 to fit, trim, and sew 4½"-wide border strips to top, bottom, and sides of quilt. Press seams toward borders.

LAYERING AND FINISHING

1. Cut backing fabric crosswise into two equal pieces. Sew pieces together on long edges to make one 65" x 84" (approximate) backing piece. Arrange and baste backing, batting, and top together, referring to Layering the Quilt directions on page 111.

2. Hand or machine quilt as desired.

3. Cut one 2¾" x 42" binding strip in half and sew halves to two 2¾" x 42" strips. Sew remaining 2¾" x 42" binding strips together in pairs. Using shorter strips for top and bottom and longer strips for sides, refer to Binding the Quilt directions on page 111 to finish.

WATERING CAN DINNERWARE

Welcome spring to your table with this delightful dinnerware adorned with watering cans and festive flowers. For information on where to buy Debbie Mumm® dinnerware, visit www.debbiemumm.com or call (888) 819-2923.

HAND·PAINTED WATERING CAN

Photo: page 49

Checks, Stripes and Dots Watering Can

A WATERING CAN BE USED FOR WATERING *your garden plants … or it can be used as a colorful accent on your patio or porch. With these quick and easy steps, you can transform a metal watering can into a piece of painted garden art.*

Daisy Watering Can

MATERIALS NEEDED

Galvanized watering can

Household vinegar

Spray metal primer

Acrylic paints

Graphite paper

Paint brush

Toothbrush

Spray varnish

 PREPARING THE WATERING CAN

1. Galvanized can needs to be washed with vinegar, rinsed well, and allowed to dry completely.

2. Spray watering can with a solid coat of spray metal primer. A light color is best.

 PAINTING THE WATERING CAN

Apply base coat colors. This will generally require two coats for complete coverage.

INSTRUCTIONS

ADDING DETAILS

Checks and stripes - On areas where checks or stripes are painted, apply lightest color first. Then paint stripes or checks over lighter base color.

Draw pattern on with a ruler and pencil to help keep lines straight. A checkerboard stencil can also be used to paint checks.

Dots - Dots on body of can are applied using the end of a paintbrush dipped in a contrasting color then dotted onto can. The larger the brush end, the larger the dot. Keep brush straight up and down and pick up fresh paint for every dot to create uniform shapes.

Daisy - Enlarge daisy template below to size that will fit can. Trace daisy onto piece of tracing paper. Using graphite paper between tracing paper and can, trace with pen over pattern onto can surface.

daisy template
enlarge to fit watering can

FINISHING TOUCHES

1. Paint all metal edges on can, spout, and handle with a contrasting color using small detail brush. Spray can with a matte finish varnish.

2. For an aged look apply an antiquing medium. Many products are available in water or oil base formulas. Follow manufacturer's instructions for best results.

3. A light splatter of dark acrylic paint will add to antique look. To apply, run thumb over a paint-filled toothbrush. Always test this on scrap paper first.

4. When dry, apply a finish coat of spray varnish. This comes in satin, matte, or gloss finishes.

GARDEN PARTY
49

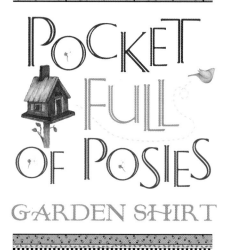

POCKET FULL OF POSIES

GARDEN SHIRT

Photo: pages 40 and 41

A FAVORITE DENIM

SHIRT CAN BE

the beginning for this cute
and comfy gardening attire.
Pockets are deep and plentiful,
just right for holding gloves,
seed packets, and other
gardening necessities.
Make one as a gift for your
favorite gardener ... then
another, just for you!

Shirt Layout

MATERIALS AND FABRIC NEEDED

Border prints and other directional fabrics require additional yardage.

Fabric A *(deep pockets)* - 1⅛ yards

Fabric B *(deep pocket accent)* - ⅙ yard

Fabric C *(pocket flap, elbow patches, hankie)* - ⅜ yard

Fabric D *(back and shoulder accent strips)* - ⅙ yard

Assorted scraps - *(front shirt pocket, patches, label)*

Long-sleeve denim shirt

Buttons for front shirt pocket and to replace buttons on shirt front and cuffs

DEEP POCKETS WITH ACCENT TRIM

1. Measure around bottom edge of shirt from one inside edge of button placket to other inside edge of button placket. Add ½" to this measurement which will be Measurement A.

2. Cut two 18½" x 42" strips from Fabric A. Sew strips together end to end to make one 18½"-wide strip.

3. Trim strip from step 2 to Measurement A as determined in step 1. Strip now measures 18½" x Measurement A.

4. Fold strip in half lengthwise, right sides together. Using ¼" seams, sew three raw (unfolded) edges, leaving an opening to turn. Clip corners, turn unit right side out, and press.

folded edge

opening to turn

Measurement A

5. Cut two 2" x 42" strips from Fabric B. Sew strips together end to end to make one 2"-wide strip.

6. Trim strip from step 5 to Measurement A as determined in step 1. Turn raw edge under ¼" on all sides and press. Pin pressed strip even with top edge of pocket unit and topstitch in place.

7. Pin pocket unit from step 6 to shirt bottom, starting along inside edge of one button placket and ending along inside edge of opposite button placket. Attach with two rows of topstitching ¼" apart along side and bottom edges.

8. Space a series of vertical lines approximately 6" apart along pocket unit. Stitch two rows of stitching (¼" apart) along these lines to form pockets.

shirt bottom edge (laid flat)

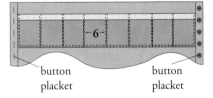

button placket   button placket

PATCH POCKET WITH HANKIE

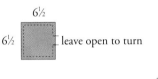

1. Cut two 6½" squares from scrap fabric. Pin squares right sides together. Using ¼" seams, sew all four sides leaving an opening to turn. Clip corners, turn unit right side out, and press.

6½

6½   leave open to turn

2. Refer to project illustration on page 50 to position and pin pocket to shirt front. Topstitch pocket in place along sides and bottom edge.

3. Cut one 12½" square from Fabric C. Hem all edges, fold, and tuck into pocket unit from step 2.

DECORATIVE POCKET

1. Measure top edge of shirt's existing breast pocket and add ½" (Measurement B). Cut two pieces of Fabric C to measurements as shown.

Measurement B

2 ▭ 2¾

2. Pin pieces right sides together. Using ¼" seams, sew all sides. Clip corners and make a small opening in one layer to allow for turning. Turn and press.

cut 1" opening

3. Pin flap to top edge of pocket and stitch in place. Secure point of flap with decorative button.

4. Cut one 3½" square from Fabric C. Turn raw edge under ¼" on all sides and press. Refer to project illustration to position patch on pocket. Stitch in place.

elbow patch pattern piece
cut 4 (seam allowance included)

1. Refer to color photo on page 41. Cut one 4¼" x 42" Fabric D strip. Measure across shirt back along shoulder line from arm seam to arm seam. Add ½" to this measurement, which will be Measurement C.

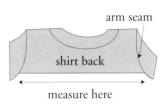

2. Trim strip from step 1 to Measurement C. Strip now measures 4¼" x Measurement C. Turn raw edge under ¼" on all sides and press. Pin to shirt back and topstitch in place.

FINISHING TOUCHES

1. Replace buttons on denim shirt with buttons in your preferred colors.

2. Cut one 3¼" square from scrap. Turn raw edge under ¼" on all sides and press. Use this patch to create your own customized label, and stitch in place over manufacturer's label in shirt collar.

ELBOW PATCHES

1. Make elbow patch template from pattern on page 52. Cut four 8" x 6" pieces from Fabric C. For each patch, position two fabric pieces right sides together, trace around template, and cut on drawn line. Using ¼" seams, sew around entire raw edge. Clip curves and make a small opening in one layer to allow for turning. Turn and press.

2. Cut two 3¼" squares from scrap fabric. Turn raw edge under ¼" on all sides of each square and press. Position one square on each elbow patch. Stitch in place.

3. Refer to shirt layout on page 50. Position one elbow patch on each shirt sleeve and sew in place.

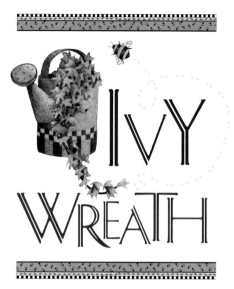

IVY WREATH

Wreath Layout

Photo: page 55

GARDEN ELEGANCE·
THAT'S WHAT YOU'LL

create with this lovely wreath of trailing ivy. Whether it graces your front porch, your summer garden, or your kitchen, it will add a truly unique accent. Pots of fresh ivy are added to a twig wreath to wind in and out, and fanciful garden ornaments give it a colorful finishing touch.

MATERIALS NEEDED

Twig wreath - 18" diameter

Three terra cotta pots - 3" planted
    with ivy

Garden ornaments - Debbie
Mumm® Ornaments from
    Creative Imaginations,
    (800) 942-6487

Craft wire - 18 gauge

Glue gun and glue sticks

Raffia

FOR ANOTHER
COUNTRY LOOK

*Make it a kitchen wreath!
Add planted pots of ivy to the
twig wreath, but for accents
use miniature kitchen
utensils and treasures, or
combine cookie cutters made
of copper or tin with vintage
measuring cups and spoons.
For inspiration visit your
favorite kitchen shop!*

GARDEN PARTY
54

INSTRUCTIONS

TO CREATE YOUR WREATH

1. Begin by placing pots of ivy in a pleasing position at bottom of twig wreath. Secure in place using glue gun. Reinforce with wire and wind ends to back of wreath.

2. Wrap ivy vines around wreath, encircling it as much as possible with vines. Refer to color photo for reference. Tuck ends of vines into wreath.

3. For a finishing touch add small garden ornaments to ivy pots and wire garden ornaments to pots and sides of wreath. Make a raffia bow and wire to bottom of wreath, referring to photo below.

4. To give your ivy a good start in its new home, be sure and fertilize it generously with an all-purpose fertilizer for house plants.

FARMHOUSE KITCHEN

THE HEART OF THE home … the farmhouse kitchen radiates warmth and hospitality to everyone who stops by for a neighborly visit. There's always room for one more at the table when a delicious country breakfast of farm-fresh eggs and hand-squeezed orange juice is served. So pull up a chair and help yourself to the irresistible fare and to the cozy warmth of this inviting country setting.

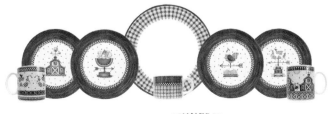

WEATHERVANE DINNERWARE

57

BARNS AND FARMS

QUILT

Finished Size: 63" x 71"

Photo: page 56

**IMAGINE A PICTURE
PERFECT COUNTRY**

*landscape, dotted with red barns,
neatly planted rows of crops, and
gaily whirling windmills ... then
bring this pleasant daydream home
with our charming Barns and Farms
quilt! Small appliqué accents add a
touch of realism to the quick-pieced
Barn Blocks, while three Windmill
Blocks are appliquéd in place to
highlight the traditional sashed set.
Read all instructions before beginning
and use ¼"-wide seams throughout.*

Quilt Layout

FABRIC REQUIREMENTS

Directional fabrics are not
recommended.

Fabric A *(barns)* - ¼ yard each of
four red fabrics

Fabric B *(sky)* - ⅝ yard

Fabric C *(four patches)* - ⅙ yard light
fabric

Fabric D *(four patches)* - ⅙ yard dark
fabric

Fabric E *(windmill blades)* - ⅙ yard

Fabric F *(windmill blades)* - ½ yard

Fabric G *(windmill background)*
⅓ yard

Crop Rows - ⅓ yard each of four
green fabrics

Frames and Timbers - ¼ yard

Doors - Four 4" x 4½" pieces

Windows - Four 2½" squares

Shutters - Eight 2½" x 1½" pieces

Roofs - Four 4½" x 8½" pieces

Sashing - 1⅓ yards

Accent Border - ⅓ yard

Border - ⅞ yard

Binding - ⅝ yard

Backing - 4 yards

Lightweight batting - 71" x 79"
piece

CUTTING THE STRIPS AND PIECES

Read first paragraph of Cutting the Strips and Pieces on page 7.

Fabric A (barns)

* One 4½" x 42" strip, cut into
  • One 4½" x 16½" piece
  • Two 4½" x 6" pieces
  • Two 2½" squares
* One 1½" x 20" strip, cut into
  • Two 1½" x 8½" pieces

Repeat for each of four fabrics.

Fabric B (sky)

* Four 4½" x 42" strips, cut into
  • Eight 4½" x 8½" pieces
  • Sixteen 4½" squares

Fabric C (four patches)

* Three 1½" x 42" strips

Fabric D (four patches)

* Three 1½" x 42" strips

Fabric E (windmill blades)

* One 4¼ " x 42" strip, cut into
  • Nine 4¼ " squares

Fabric F (windmill blades)

* Four 3⅛" x 42" strips

Fabric G (windmill background)

* One 4¼ " x 42" strip, cut into
  • Nine 4¼ " squares
* Four 1¼ " x 42" strips

Crop Rows

* Five 2" x 42" strips

Repeat for each of four fabrics.

Frames and Timbers

* Two 1½" x 42" strips, cut into
  • Eight 1½" x 8" pieces
  (roof timbers)
* Four 1" x 42" strips, cut into
  • Four 1" x 8" pieces
  (roof timbers)
  • Eight 1" x 6" pieces
  (door timbers)
  • Twelve 1" x 4½" pieces
  (door frames)

Sashing

* Seventeen 2½" x 42" strips, cut into
  • Six 2½" x 34½" strips
  • Ten 2½" x 16½" strips
  • Thirty-six 2½" x 6½" pieces

Accent Border

* Seven 1" x 42" strips

Border

* Seven 4" x 42" strips

Binding

* Seven 2¾" x 42" strips

MAKING THE BLOCKS

You'll be making four Barn Blocks that will measure 16½" and nine sashed Windmill Blocks that will measure 10½".

Whenever possible, use the assembly line method for each step. Position pieces right sides together and line up next to your sewing machine. Stitch first unit together, then continue sewing others without breaking threads. When all units are sewn, clip threads to separate them. Press in direction of arrows in diagrams.

BARN BLOCKS

1. Machine stitch or refer to Hand Appliqué directions on page 110. Appliqué two 1" x 6" door timber pieces to form an "x" over each 4½" x 4"door piece as shown. Trim edges of appliquéd pieces even with edges of fabric. Make a total of four.

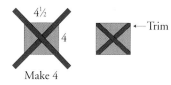

Make 4   ←Trim

2. Sew one 1" x 4½" door frame piece to top edge of each unit from step 1.

Make 4

3. Arrange and sew one unit from step 2, two 1" x 4½" door frame pieces, and two matching 4½" x 6" Fabric A pieces as shown. Press. Make a total of four.

Make 4

4. Refer to Quick Corner Triangle directions on page 110. Sew two 4½" Fabric B squares to each 4½" x 16½" Fabric A piece. Press. Make a total of four.

A = 4½ x 16½
B = 4½ x 4½
Make 4

5. Sew units from step 3 to matching units from step 4 in pairs as shown. Press. Make four.

Make 4

6. Arrange and sew two matching 2½" Fabric A squares, two 2½" x 1½" shutter pieces, and one 2½" window square as shown. Press. Make a total of four.

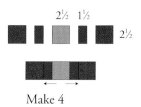

Make 4

7. Sew each unit from step 6 between two matching 1½" x 8½" Fabric A pieces. Press. Make four.

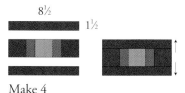

Make 4

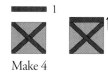

BARNS AND FARMS QUILT   DEBBIE MUMM'S• COUNTRY SETTINGS

8. Refer to Quick Corner Triangle directions on page 110. Sew two remaining 4½" Fabric B squares to each 4½" x 8½" roof piece. Press. Make a total of four.

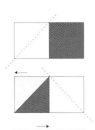

Roof = 4½ x 8½
B = 4½ x 4½
Make 4

9. Sew units from step 7 to units from step 8 in pairs as shown. Press. Make four.

Make 4

10. Sew each unit from step 9 between two 4½" x 8½" Fabric B pieces. Press. Make a total of four.

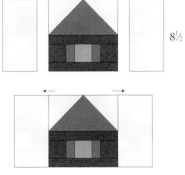

4½

8½

Make 4

11. Sew units from step 5 to matching units from step 10 in pairs as shown. Press. Block will measure 16½" square.

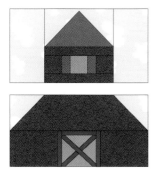 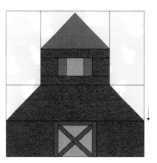

Make 4

12. Refer to project layout on page 58. Machine stitch or refer to Hand Appliqué directions on page 110. Appliqué one 1" x 8" timber piece at base and two 1½" x 8" timber pieces over peak of each roof.

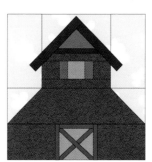

Make 4

 FOUR PATCH BLOCKS

1. Sew 1½" x 42" Fabric C and 1½" x 42" Fabric D strips in pairs to make three strip sets measuring 2½" x 42". Press seams toward darker fabrics. Using rotary cutter and ruler, cut a total of seventy-two 1½" segments from strip sets.

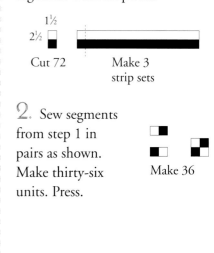

2. Sew segments from step 1 in pairs as shown. Make thirty-six units. Press.

Make 36

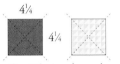

WINDMILL BLOCKS

1. Cut each 4¼" Fabric E square in half twice diagonally to make thirty-six triangles. Repeat, using 4¼" Fabric G squares.

Cut 36 triangles each

2. Sew Fabric E and G triangles from step 1 in pairs along one short side to make thirty-six two-triangle units as shown. Press.

Make 36

3. Sew 3⅛" x 42" Fabric F and 1¼" x 42" Fabric G strips in pairs to make four strip sets. Press. Using rotary cutter and ruler, cut a total of thirty-six 3⅞" segments from the strip sets.

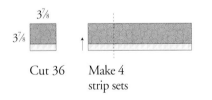

Cut 36   Make 4
                  strip sets

4. Cut each 3⅞" segment from step 3 in half once diagonally to make two triangles. The triangles labeled * will be used to complete the blocks.

*Use this triangle

5. Sew triangle units from step 2 to triangle units from step 4 in pairs along their long edges. Press. Make a total of thirty-six.

Make 36

6. Sew units from step 5 together in pairs as shown. Press. Make a total of eighteen.

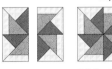

Make 18

7. Sew units from step 6 together in pairs as shown. Press. Make nine.

Make 9

Nostalgia is remembering the pleasures of our old kitchen when we were kids, without remembering how long it took to wash the dishes.

Caroline Brownlow

from the book
Tea Time Friends
Brownlow©1999
illustrated by Debbie Mumm®

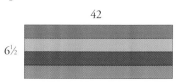

CROP ROWS

1. Sew one each of four different 2" x 42" green strips together to make a strip set measuring 6½" x 42". Press. Make five strip sets. Using rotary cutter and ruler, cut one 34½" segment from each of three strip sets, and two 16½" segments from each of two remaining strip sets.

42

6½

Make 5 strip sets

2. Sew each 6½" x 34½" segment from step 1 between two 2½" x 34½" sashing strips. Press seams toward sashing strips. Make three. Repeat to sew each 6½" x 16½" segment from step 1 between two 2½" x 16½" sashing strips. Press. Make four.

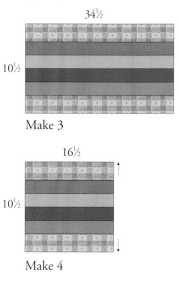

34½

10½

Make 3

16½

10½

Make 4

8. Sew each Windmill unit from step 7 between two 2½" x 6½" sashing strips. Press. Make a total of nine.

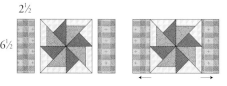

2½

6½

Make 9

9. Sew each remaining 2½" x 6½" sashing strip between two four-patch blocks as shown. Press. Make eighteen.

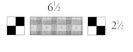

6½

2½

Make 18

10. Sew each unit from step 8 between two units from step 9. Press. Make nine. Block will measure 10½" square.

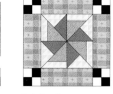

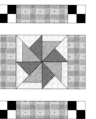

Make 9

=Baaa

FARMHOUSE KITCHEN

64

1. Arrange two Barn Blocks, two 16½" sashed Crop Rows, and one 2½" x 16½" sashing strip in a horizontal row as shown. Sew the blocks, sashed rows, and sashing strip together. Press seams away from Barn Blocks. Make two rows.

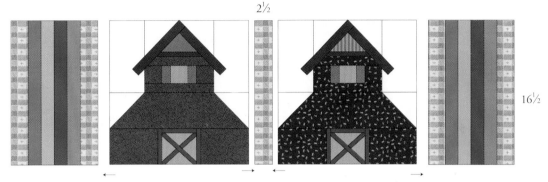

2½

16½

Make 2 rows

2. Sew each 34½" sashed Crop Row between two Windmill Blocks as shown. Press seams away from Windmill Blocks. Make three rows.

Make 3 rows

3. Referring to project layout on page 58, arrange rows in their proper order. Join rows and press.

4. Cut one 1" x 42" accent border strip in half and sew halves to two accent border strips. Measure quilt through center from side to side. Trim strips to this measurement. Sew to top and bottom. Press toward accent border.

5. Sew remaining accent border strips together in pairs. Measure quilt through center from top to bottom. Trim strips to this measurement. Sew to sides. Press.

6. Repeat steps 4 and 5 for measuring and add 4" borders to quilt in same manner.

7. Machine stitch or refer to Hand Appliqué directions on page 110. Turn each remaining Windmill Block on point and appliqué in place as shown in the project layout on page 58.

Cock-a-doodle-do!

LAYERING AND FINISHING

1. Cut backing fabric crosswise into two equal pieces. Sew pieces together on long edges to make one 72" x 84" (approximate) backing piece. Arrange and baste backing, batting, and top together, referring to Layering the Quilt directions on page 111.

2. Machine or hand quilt as desired.

3. Cut one 2¾" x 42" binding strip in half and sew halves to two 2¾" x 42" strips. Sew remaining 2¾" x 42" binding strips together in pairs. Using shorter strips for top and bottom and longer strips for sides, refer to Binding the Quilt directions on page 111 to finish.

Good Mornin'!

© Debbie Mumm

WEATHERVANE DINNERWARE

Deep shades of barn red and warm gold set the tone for this delightful collection of Americana barns and farm designs. Truly a unique dinnerware collection! For information on where to buy Debbie Mumm® dinnerware, visit www.debbiemumm.com or call (888) 819-2923.

CHICKEN SOUP

PLACEMAT

Finished Size: 14½" square

Photo: page 57

WHETHER IT'S

BREAKFAST, LUNCH, OR

*dinner, this charming chicken adds
rustic charm to any mealtime. Ours
is hand appliquéd, but you can
substitute the quick-fuse method if
you prefer. Fabric requirements and
cutting instructions are for a single
placemat; make as many as you need
for your country table. Read all
instructions before beginning and use
¼"-wide seams throughout.*

Placemat Layout

FABRIC REQUIREMENTS

ONE PLACEMAT:

Background - 8½" square

Appliqués - Assorted scraps for
   feet, body, wing, face, comb

Inside Border - ⅛ yard

Middle Border - ⅛ yard

Outside Border - ⅙ yard

Backing - 15" square

Low-loft batting - 15" square

Embroidery floss

INSTRUCTIONS

CUTTING THE STRIPS AND PIECES

Read first paragraph of Cutting the Strips and Pieces on page 7.

Inside Border
* One 1½" x 42" strip, cut into
  • Two 1½" x 8½" strips
  • Two 1½" x 10½" strips

Middle Border
* Two 1" x 42" strips, cut into
  • Two 1" x 10½" strips
  • Two 1" x 11½" strips

Outside Border
* Two 2¼" x 42" strips, cut into
  • Two 2¼" x 11½" strips
  • Two 2¼" x 15" strips

PREPARING FOR APPLIQUÉ

1. Trace appliqué designs from page 70. Make templates and use assorted scraps to trace one each of pieces 1 (feet), 2 (body), 3 (wing), 4 (comb), 5 (head), and 6 (face and eye). Cut out appliqués, adding ¼" seam allowance around each piece.

2. Fold 8½" background block in half on both diagonals and press lightly to find centerpoint. Referring to placement diagram on page 68, turn block on point and position appliqués. Use preferred method to stitch appliqués in place.

3. Referring to pattern on page 70 for placement, use two strands of embroidery floss to make French knot eye and three strands of floss to embroider beak. Refer to Embroidery Stitch Guide on page 110.

FARMHOUSE KITCHEN
69

BORDERS

Sew short inside border strips to two opposite sides of block. Press seams away from block. Sew long inside border strips to two remaining sides of block. Press. Repeat to add middle and then outside borders to all four sides of block. Press.

LAYERING AND FINISHING

1. Position top and backing right sides together. Center both pieces on top of batting and pin all three layers together. Using ¼" seams, sew around edges, leaving an opening for turning.

2. Trim backing and batting to same size as top. Trim corners, turn right side out, hand stitch opening closed, and press.

3. Machine or hand quilt as desired.

appliqué pattern pieces
Chicken Soup Placemat

MAKE IT A WALLHANGING

Our Chicken Soup Placemat will bring a whimsical touch to your kitchen table, but that's not the only spot you can use it.

How about on your kitchen wall? Our fun and friendly chicken can be the perfect accent to your décor when you create it in colors that coordinate with your kitchen.

We've created ours in rich tones of black and red, but it will have an entirely different personality when you make it from bright, bold tones ... or even from an assortment of your favorite scraps. Any way you make it, Chicken Soup is always "just what the doctor ordered!"

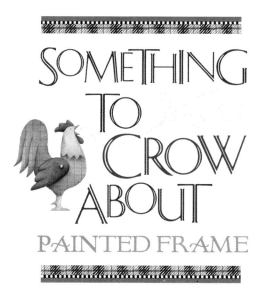

SOMETHING TO CROW ABOUT

PAINTED FRAME

Photo: page 73

YOU'LL REALLY HAVE "SOMETHING TO CROW

about" when you create this lovely country-style wooden frame to showcase a favorite print. With our careful step-by-step instructions, you can easily paint this unique accent in colors that will highlight your own home décor.

Frame Layout

MATERIALS NEEDED

Frame - unfinished wood

Liner brush and #2 flat brush

Sponge brush

Tracing paper and graphite paper

Graphite pencil or white chalk pencil

Scotch™ Magic™ Tape *(no substitution recommended)*

Antiquing medium

Matte craft varnish

Acrylic paints - red, gold, green, black, ivory, tan

Sandpaper

Debbie Mumm® "A Little Something to Crow About" - print from Wild Apple Graphics, (800) 756-8359

PAINTING THE FRAME

1. Paint flat surface of frame with a thin wash of red paint. Allow it to dry completely for several hours or overnight.

2. Sand lightly to smooth surface.

3. Draw a line ⅛" around frame opening using a graphite or white chalk pencil.

4. Place tape on outside edge of pencil line. Press firmly.

INSTRUCTIONS

5. Using edge of tape as a stencil line, paint the strip along inside edge with ivory.

6. With a ruler and the tape still in place, measure and draw ⅛" checks using a pencil to mark border.

7. Paint every other check black. Sand lightly to give an antiqued look. Remove tape.

8. Measure and draw a guideline ⅜" from outside edge of frame. Apply tape along inside of drawn edge. Press firmly.

9. Paint along edge with tan. Leave tape in place and lightly sponge with ivory over tan to give a mottled look. Remove tape.

10. Trace pattern for vine and corner pieces onto a piece of tracing paper. Using graphite paper between tracing paper and wood, trace with a pen over pattern onto wood surface. Do this for vine and corner pieces.

11. Using liner brush and dark green paint slightly thinned, paint vine and leaf pattern. Let dry. To give an antiqued look, lightly sand.

12. Using diagram as a guide, paint corner pieces with gold, green, red, and tan.

13. Paint outside edge of frame green. Paint inside edge of frame red.

14. Spray lightly with a matte craft varnish. Antique following directions on a purchased antiquing medium.

15. When dry spray again with a matte varnish.

MORE OPTIONS:

A very simple frame could be achieved by using different techniques such as sponging, crackling, or simple staining. Any of these techniques combined with a simple checked border will help you create a delightful frame for any favorite print.

•

It's easy to create a fabric-covered mat to match your print.
First, cut a piece of mat board and fabric slightly larger than the finished size of the mat. Apply fusible web to the wrong side of the fabric according to manufacturer's instructions. Remove the paper and iron onto the mat board. Be sure the fabric is adhered well to the mat board, then cut the mat to the desired size.

frame template
enlarge to fit frame

COUNTRY VINTAGE KITCHEN

WARM, FRESHLY baked bread ... close your eyes and you can almost smell its irresistible aroma when you step into this country vintage kitchen. This charming setting with its quilts of red, blue, and yellow brings back wonderful memories of sitting around the stove at grandma's house. For just a short while, slow down life's busy pace and enjoy a nostalgic visit to yesterday.

COUNTRY VINTAGE KITCHEN DINNERWARE

75

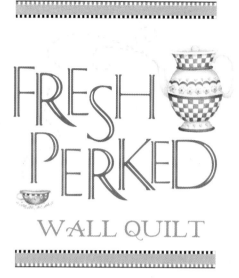

FRESH PERKED
WALL QUILT

Finished Size: 39" square

Photo: page 74

M-M-M-M! JAVA JOE, CAFE-
YOU'LL ALMOST SMELL

*the coffee beans roasting as you stitch
this delightful tribute to
America's favorite morning brew!
Quick-pieced construction leaves you
time to spare – perfect for settling
in with your favorite mug, a
tasty treat, and that new quilting
book you've longed to browse.
Read all instructions before
beginning and use ¼"-wide
seams throughout.*

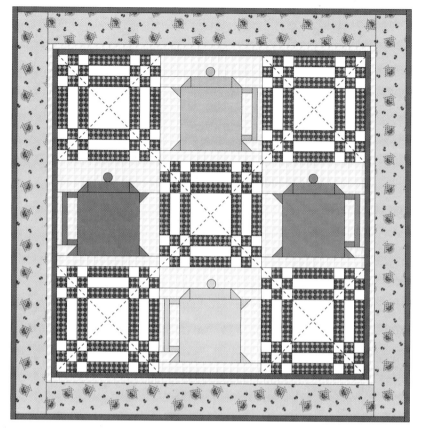

Quilt Layout

FABRIC REQUIREMENTS

Directional fabrics are
not recommended.

Fabric A *(coffee pots)* - ¼ yard each
of four fabrics

Fabric B *(background)* - ½ yard

Fabric C *(checkerboard blocks)*
½ yard of dark fabric

Fabric D *(checkerboard blocks)*
⅝ yard of light fabric

First Accent Border - ⅙ yard

Second Accent Border - ⅙ yard

Border - ½ yard

Backing - 1¼ yards

Binding - ⅜ yard

Lightweight batting - 43" square

Buttons - Four ⅞"

Embroidery floss

INSTRUCTIONS

CUTTING THE STRIPS AND PIECES

Read first paragraph of Cutting the Strips and Pieces on page 7.

Fabric A (coffee pots)

* One 6½" square
* One 1½" x 14" strip, cut into
  * One 1½" x 4½" piece
  * Five 1½" squares
* One 1" x 10" strip, cut into
  * One 1" x 5½" piece
  * Two 1" x 1½" pieces

Repeat for each of four fabrics.

Fabric B (background)

* Two 2½" x 42" strips, cut into
  * Four 2½" x 10½" pieces
  * Four 2½" x 6½" pieces
* Three 1½" x 42" strips, cut into
  * Four 1½" x 10½" pieces
  * Four 1½" x 4½" pieces
  * Eight 1½" x 3½" pieces
  * Four 1½" x 2½" pieces
* One 1" x 24" strip, cut into
  * Four 1" x 5½" pieces

Fabric C (checkerboard blocks)

* Ten 1½" x 42" strips

Fabric D (checkerboard blocks)

* One 4½" x 42" strip, cut into
  * Five 4½" squares
* Eight 1½" x 42" strips

First Accent Border
* Four 1" x 42" strips

Second Accent Border
* Four 1" x 42" strips

Border
* Four 3½" x 42" strips

Binding
* Five 2¾" x 42" strips

MAKING THE BLOCKS

You'll be making four Coffee Pot Blocks and five Checkerboard Blocks.

COFFEE POT BLOCKS

For all blocks, refer to Quick Corner Triangle directions on page 110.

1. Sew two 1½" Fabric A squares to each 2½" x 6½" Fabric B piece as shown. Press. Make a total of four.

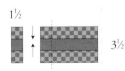

Cut 4

2. Sew one 1½" x 4½" Fabric B piece between two 1" x 1½" Fabric A pieces. Press. Make a total of four.

Make 4

3. Sew one 1" x 5½" Fabric A piece between one unit from step 2 and one 1" x 5½" Fabric B piece. Press. Make a total of four.

Make 4

4. Sew a 1½" Fabric A square to short left side of a 1½" x 2½" Fabric B piece. Press. Make two. Repeat to sew a 1½" Fabric A square to short right side of remaining 1½" x 2½" Fabric B pieces. Press. Make two.

A = 1½ x 1½
B = 1½ x 2½
Make 2 of each

5. Sew one unit from step 4 to bottom edge of each unit from step 3. Be sure step 3 units are positioned as shown. Press. Make two of each.

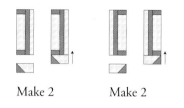

Make 2   Make 2

6. Sew one 6½" Fabric A square between one unit from step 1 and one unit from step 5. Be sure step 1 and step 5 units are positioned as shown. Press. Make two of each.

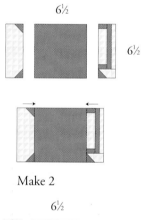

6½

6½   6½

Make 2

6½

6½   6½

Make 2

7. Sew a 1½" Fabric A square to the short right side of a 1½" x 3½" Fabric B piece. Press. Make four. Repeat to sew a 1½" Fabric A square to the short left side of remaining 1½" x 3½" Fabric B pieces. Press. Make a total of four.

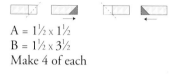

A = 1½ x 1½
B = 1½ x 3½
Make 4 of each

8. Sew one 1½" x 4½" Fabric A piece between two opposite units from step 7 as shown. Press. Make a total of four.

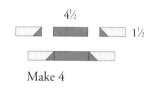

4½

1½

Make 4

9. Sew one 2½" x 10½" Fabric B piece, one unit from step 8, one unit from step 6, and one 1½" x 10½" Fabric B strip in order as shown. Press. Make two of each. Block will measure 10½" square.

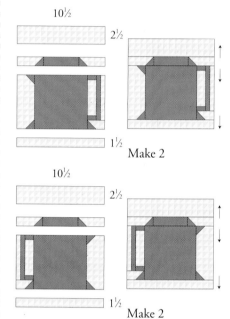

10½

2½

1½
Make 2

10½

2½

1½
Make 2

CHECKERBOARD BLOCKS

1. Sew one 1½" x 42" Fabric C strip between two 1½" x 42" Fabric D strips to make a strip set that measures 3½" x 42". Press. Make two strip sets. Using rotary cutter and ruler, cut forty 1½" segments from strip sets.

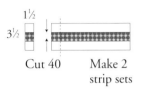

Cut 40   Make 2 strip sets

2. Sew one 1½" x 42" Fabric D strip between two 1½" x 42" Fabric C strips to make a strip set that measures 3½" x 42". Press. Make four strip sets. Using rotary cutter and ruler, cut twenty 1½" segments from one strip set.

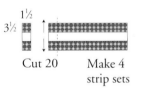

Cut 20   Make 4 strip sets

3. Sew one segment from step 2 between two segments from step 1 as shown. Press. Make twenty.

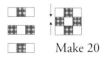

Make 20

4. Using rotary cutter and ruler, cut twenty 4½" segments from remaining strip sets from step 2.

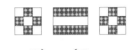

Cut 20

5. Sew one segment from step 4 between two units from step 3 as shown. Press. Make a total of ten.

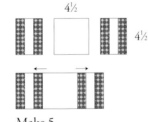

Make 10

6. Sew each 4½" Fabric D square between two segments from step 4. Press. Make a total of five.

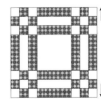

Make 5

7. Sew one unit from step 6 between two units from step 5. Press. Make a total of five. Block will measure 10½" square.

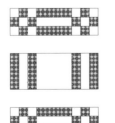

Make 5

USE YOUR VINTAGE LINENS

Maybe they're tucked away in a cupboard drawer or in an old attic trunk. Wherever you've stashed them, bring out those vintage napkins and use them! These treasures are much too lovely to be hidden away.

They add a delightful accent to a kitchen shelf when a corner is draped over the edge. Use them just as they are or sew on a bright fabric border to match your dinnerware and add your own hand embroidery.

To embroider the vintage-looking coffee pot seen in the photo on page 81, use the template on page 95 for an embroidery guide.

79

ASSEMBLY

1. Referring to project layout on page 76, arrange blocks into three horizontal rows of three alternating blocks. Rows 1 and 3 begin with Checkerboard Blocks. Row 2 begins with a Coffee Pot Block. Sew blocks into rows. Press seams toward Checkerboard Blocks.

2. Sew rows together. Press.

3. Measure quilt through center from side to side. Trim two 1" x 42" first accent border strips to this measurement. Sew to top and bottom. Press seams toward accent border.

4. Measure quilt through center from top to bottom, including border. Trim strips to this measurement. Sew to sides. Press.

5. Measure, trim, and add 1" second accent borders, and then 3½" borders in same manner.

LAYERING AND FINISHING

1. Arrange and baste backing, batting, and top together, referring to Layering the Quilt directions on page 111.

2. Machine or hand quilt as desired.

3. Cut one 2¾" x 42" binding strip in half and sew halves to two 2¾" x 42" strips. Using shorter strips for top and bottom and longer (pieced) strips for sides, refer to Binding the Quilt directions on page 111 to finish.

4. Refer to project layout and Embroidery Stitch Guide on page 110. Embroider running stitch through center of each block. Sew buttons to coffee pot lids.

COUNTRY VINTAGE
KITCHEN DINNERWARE

Tiny red and white checks border the charming kitchen images from yesterday in this nostalgic dinnerware. For information on where to buy Debbie Mumm® dinnerware, visit www.debbiemumm.com or call (888) 819-2923.

CHECKER BOARD CHURN DASH

TABLE QUILT

Finished Size: 50" square

Photo: page 85

WHETHER YOU LIVE

IN A 100-YEAR-OLD

farmhouse or a sleek city condo, this updated version of the cozy Churn Dash pattern will feel right at home. High-contrast fabrics add punch to the crisp checkerboard bars, cut and pieced effortlessly from efficient strip-sets. You'll love our all-in-one method for adding mitered borders! Read all instructions before beginning and use ¼"-wide seams throughout.

Quilt Layout

FABRIC REQUIREMENTS

Fabric A *(corner triangles)* - ¼ yard each of four yellow fabrics

Fabric B *(background)* - ½ yard each of four blue fabrics

Fabric C *(checkerboard)* - ½ yard light fabric

Fabric D *(checkerboard)* - ½ yard red fabric

Accent Border - ¼ yard

Middle Border - ¼ yard

Outside Border - ⅝ yard

Binding - ½ yard

Backing - 3 yards

Lightweight batting - 54" square

INSTRUCTIONS

CUTTING THE STRIPS AND PIECES

Read first paragraph of Cutting the Strips and Pieces on page 7.

Fabric A *(corner triangles)*
* Two 3½" x 42" strips, cut into
  • Sixteen 3½" squares

Repeat for each of four fabrics.

Fabric B *(background)*
* One 4½" x 42" strip, cut into
  • Four 4½" squares
* Two 3½" x 42" strips, cut into
  • Sixteen 3½" squares
* Two 1½" x 42" strips, cut into
  • Sixteen 1½" x 4½" pieces

Repeat for each of four fabrics.

Fabric C *(checkerboard)*
* Ten 1½" x 42" strips

Fabric D *(checkerboard)*
* Ten 1½" x 42" strips

Accent Border
* Five 1" x 42" strips

Middle Border
* Five 1½" x 42" strips

Outside Border
* Five 3½" x 42" strips

Binding
* Six 2¾" x 42" strips

MAKING THE BLOCKS

You will be making sixteen Checkerboard Churn Dash Blocks.

Whenever possible, use the assembly line method for each step. Position pieces right sides together and line up next to your sewing machine. Stitch first unit together, then continue sewing others without breaking threads. When all units are sewn, clip threads to separate them. Press in direction of arrows in diagrams.

CHECKERBOARD CHURN DASH BLOCKS

1. Alternate fabrics and sew two 1½" x 42" Fabric C and two 1½" x 42" Fabric D strips together to make a strip set that measures 4½" x 42". Press seams toward darker fabrics. Make five strip sets. Using rotary cutter and ruler, cut one hundred twenty-eight 1½" segments from strip sets.

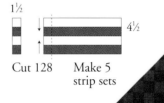

Cut 128   Make 5 strip sets

2. Sew one 1½" x 4½" Fabric B piece and two units from step 1 as shown. Press. Make sixty-four units.

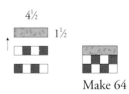

Make 64

3. Refer to Quick Corner Triangle directions on page 110. Using 3½" Fabric A and B squares, make sixty-four units. Press.

A = 3½ x 3½
B = 3½ x 3½
Make 64

4. Sew one unit from step 2 between two matching units from step 3. Press. Make thirty-two.

Make 32

5. Sew one 4½" Fabric B square between two matching units from step 2. Press. Make sixteen.

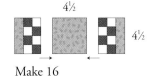

4½

4½

Make 16

6. Sew one unit from step 5 between two matching units from step 4 as shown. Press. Make sixteen. Block will measure 10½" square.

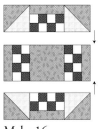

Make 16

ASSEMBLY

1. Arrange blocks in a pleasing arrangement of four horizontal rows with four blocks each. Sew blocks into rows. Press seams in opposite directions from row to row.

2. Sew rows together. Press.

MAKING AND ADDING THE MITERED BORDERS

1. Cut one 1" x 42" accent border strip into four equal pieces. Sew one piece to each remaining 1" x 42" accent border strip. Repeat to cut and piece 1½" middle border strips and 3½" outside border strips.

2. Sew one 1½" middle border strip between one 1" accent border strip and one 3½" outside border strip. Make four identical border units.

3. Measure quilt vertically and horizontally. Measurements should be the same. If they differ slightly, determine their average.

4. Fold each border unit crosswise to find its midpoint and mark with a pin. Using quilt dimension measured in step 3, measure each border unit from its midpoint and pin-mark border ends to show where edges of quilt will be.

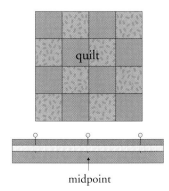

quilt

midpoint

5. Beginning at a marked end point, draw a 45 degree diagonal line to represent mitered seam line. Repeat on opposite end of strip, drawing a mirror-image diagonal line. Repeat for all four border units.

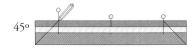

45°

6. Align a border unit to quilt with 1" inside border closest to quilt center. Pin at midpoints and pin-marked ends first, and then along entire side easing if necessary to fit.

7. Sew border to quilt, stopping and starting with a backstitch ¼" from pin-marked end points. Do not sew past pin marks at either end. Repeat to sew all four border units to quilt.

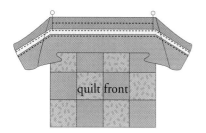

quilt front

8. Fold one corner diagonally, right sides together, matching and pinning marked diagonal sewing lines. End points of adjacent seams should match. Begin sewing with a backstitch at point where side seams ended. Sew to end of marked line at outside edge of strip. Trim excess border ¼" from seam and press open. Repeat on remaining corners.

fold
back of quilt
← trim
¼
stitch

LAYERING AND FINISHING

1. Cut backing fabric crosswise into two equal pieces. Sew pieces together on the long edges to make one 54" x 84" (approximate) backing piece. Arrange and baste backing, batting, and top together, referring to Layering the Quilt directions on page 111.

2. Hand or machine quilt as desired.

3. Cut two 2¾" x 42" binding strips in half. Sew one piece to each remaining 2¾" x 42" binding strip. Refer to Binding the Quilt directions on page 111 to finish.

VINTAGE COUNTRY

TABLE RUNNER

Finished Size: 17" x 42½"

Photo: page 87

SET THE PERFECT COUNTRY TABLE

with this checkerboard of patchwork and embroidery. No need to fret over the unusual shape – a simple pillow-turn technique makes finishing a snap! Read all instructions before beginning and use ¼"-wide seams throughout.

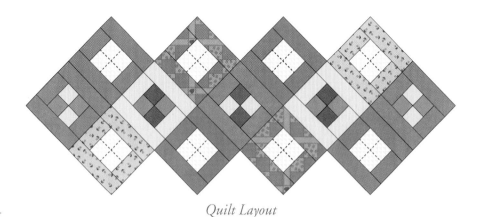

Quilt Layout

FABRIC REQUIREMENTS

Fabric A *(block 1)* - One 2" x 6" strip of ten different fabrics

Fabric B *(block 1)* - ¼ yard red fabric and ⅛ yard yellow fabric

Fabric C *(block 2)* - ⅛ yard light fabric

Fabric D *(block 2)* - ¼ yard each of green and blue fabric

Backing - (minimum 44"-wide) ⅝ yard

Flannel or lightweight batting 19" x 44" piece

Embroidery floss - Assorted colors

CUTTING THE STRIPS AND PIECES

Read first paragraph of Cutting the Strips and Pieces on page 7.

Fabric B *(block 1)*

✳ Two 2" x 42" strips, cut into
  • Six 2" x 6½" pieces (red)
  • Six 2" x 3½" pieces (red)

✳ One 2" x 42" strip, cut into
  • Four 2" x 6½" pieces (yellow)
  • Four 2" x 3½" pieces (yellow)

Fabric C

✳ One 3½" x 42" strip, cut into

  • Eight 3½" squares

Fabric D *(block 2)*

✳ Three 2" x 42" strips, cut into

  • Eight 2" x 6½" pieces (green)

  • Eight 2" x 3½" pieces (green)

Repeat for blue fabric.

MAKING THE BLOCKS

You will be making thirteen "framed" blocks: five Block One and eight Block Two. Block One is a scrappy four-patch surrounded by a red or yellow "frame." Block Two is a single, light-colored center square embellished with embroidery floss and surrounded by a green or blue frame.

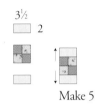

BLOCK ONE

1. Sew 2" x 6" Fabric A strips in pairs to make five 3½" x 6" strip sets. Press seams toward darker fabrics. Using rotary cutter and ruler, cut two 2" strip segments from each strip set.

2

3½

Cut 2   Make 5
strip sets

2. Sew matching segments into pairs as shown. Make five units. Press.

Make 5

3. Sew one unit from step 2 between two matching 2" x 3½" Fabric B strips. Press toward Fabric B strips. Make five.

3½
    2

Make 5

4. Sew one unit from step 3 between two matching 2" x 6½" Fabric B strips. Press seams toward Fabric B strips. Make five. Block will measure 6½" square.

2

6½

Make 5

BLOCK TWO

1. Sew one 3½" Fabric C square between two matching 2" x 3½" Fabric D strips. Press seams toward Fabric D strips. Make eight.

3½

2

3½

Make 8

2. Sew one unit from step 1 between two matching 2" x 6½" Fabric D strips. Press seams toward Fabric D strips. Make eight. Block will measure 6½" square.

2

6½

Make 8

3. Refer to project layout on page 86 and Embroidery Stitch Guide on page 110. Use three strands of embroidery floss and a running stitch to embroider a cross through center of each Fabric C square, creating an embroidered four-patch.

ASSEMBLY

1. Refer to diagram below. Arrange, alternating Block One and Block Two units in five rows, staggering rows as shown.

2. Sew blocks together into rows. Press seams in opposite directions from row to row.

3. Sew rows together, stopping and starting with a backstitch ¼" from raw edges. Press.

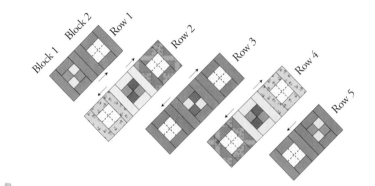

Block 1 Block 2 Row 1 Row 2 Row 3 Row 4 Row 5

LAYERING AND FINISHING

1. Position top and backing right sides together. Center both pieces on top of batting and pin all three layers together. Using ¼" seam, sew around angled edges of top, leaving an opening for turning.

2. Trim backing and batting to same size as top. Trim corners, turn right side out, hand stitch opening closed, and press.

3. Machine or hand quilt as desired.

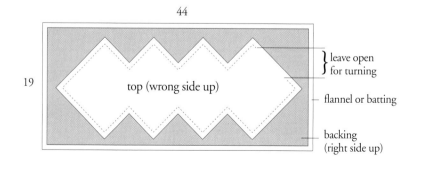

44

19

top (wrong side up)

} leave open for turning

flannel or batting

backing (right side up)

MEET OUR
KITCHEN ANGEL

Do you ever wish you had just a little good luck in the kitchen when you're creating that chocolate soufflé? Now you have it! Our very special Kitchen Angel is here to dust your kitchen with a generous sprinkling of good luck!

Bringing her into your cozy kitchen setting will make everything just a little better ... your cookies will be done just right in the middle, your salads crisp and fresh, and your pasta perfectly "al dente." Here's a little advice: Don't throw away your timer ... just in case!

My KITCHEN ANGEL

LITTLE WALL QUILTS

Checks and Dashes

Cutting Corners

Nine Patch

Each Finished Quilt Size: 11" square

Photo: page 81

DON'T BE FOOLED BY THEIR LITTLE

measurements! This trio of diminutive quilts delivers a large serving of decorative impact … in record time. Betcha can't make just one! Read all instructions before beginning and use ¼"-wide seams throughout.

FABRIC REQUIREMENTS

	Checks and Dashes	Nine Patch	Cutting Corners
Fabric A	⅙ yard *(center and checkerboard)*	One 4½" square *(center)*	One 6½" square *(center)*
Fabric B	⅛ yard *(checkerboard and border)*	⅛ yard *(nine-patch center and borders)*	¼ yard *(second strips and borders)*
Fabric C	⅛ yard *(background)*	⅛ yard *(nine-patch corner blocks and strip sets)*	¼ yard *(first strips and corners)*
Fabric D	⅛ yard *(inside corners)*	⅛ yard *(nine-patch corner blocks and strip sets)*	⅛ yard *(center triangles)*
For each quilt:	✳ Backing - 15" square ✳ Lightweight batting - 15" square piece ✳ Embroidery floss		

CUTTING THE STRIPS AND PIECES

	Checks and Dashes	Nine Patch	Cutting Corners
Fabric A	One 4½" square Two 1½" x16" strips		
Fabric B	Two 1½" x 16" strips Two 1" x 10½" strips Two 1" x 11½" strips	One 1½" x 8" strip Two 1" x 10½" strips Two 1" x 11½" strips	One 8½" square Two 1" x 10½" strips Two 1" x 11½" strips
Fabric C	One 3½" x 16" strip cut into • Four 3½" squares One 1½" x 20" strip cut into • Four 1½" x 4½ " pieces	Two 1½" x 42" strips cut into • Two 1½" x 20" strips • One 1½" x 16" strip • Two 1½" x 8" strips	One 1½" x 42" strip cut into • Two 1½" x 8½" strips • Two 1½" x 6½" strips One 3½" x 42" strip cut into • Four 3½" squares
Fabric D	One 3½" x 42" strip cut into • Four 3½" squares	Two 1½" x 42" strips cut into • One 1½" x 20" strip • Two 1½" x 16" strips	One 3½" x 42" strip cut into • Four 3½" squares

CHECKS AND DASHES

1. Alternate fabric and sew two 1½" x 16" Fabric A and Fabric B strips together to make one 4½" x 16" strip set. Press seams toward darker fabrics. Using rotary cutter and ruler, cut eight 1½" segments from strip set.

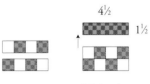

1½

4½

Cut 8

2. Sew segments in pairs as shown to make four units. Press. Then sew one 1½" x 4½" Fabric C piece to each unit. Press.

4½

1½

Make 4

3. Refer to Quick Corner Triangle directions on page 110. Using 3½" Fabric C and Fabric D squares, make four units. Press.

C = 3½ x 3½
D = 3½ x 3½
Make 4

4. Sew one unit from step 2 between two units from step 3. Press. Make two.

Make 2

5. Sew 4½" Fabric A square between remaining units from step 2. Press.

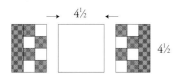

4½

4½

6. Sew unit from step 5 between units from step 4 as shown. Press. Block will measure 10½" square.

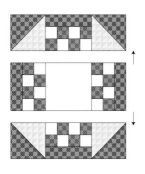

7. Sew 1" x 10½" Fabric B strips to top and bottom of block. Press seams toward border strips. Sew 1" x 11½" strips to sides. Press.

8. Trace embroidery pattern on page 95 onto Fabric A block center. Refer to Embroidery Stitch Guide on page 110. Use embroidery floss to embroider as desired.

LAYERING AND FINISHING

1. Position top and backing right sides together. Center both pieces on top of batting and pin all three layers together. Using ¼" seam, sew around edges leaving an opening for turning.

2. Trim backing and batting to same size as top. Trim corners, turn right side out, hand stitch opening closed, and press.

3. Machine or hand quilt as desired.

NINE PATCH

1. Sew 1½" x 8" Fabric B strip between two 1½" x 8" Fabric C strips to make one 3½" x 8" strip set. Press seams toward darker fabrics. Using rotary cutter and ruler, cut four 1½" segments from strip set.

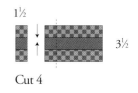

1½

3½

Cut 4

2. Sew one 1½" x 16" Fabric C strip between two 1½" x 16" Fabric D strips to make one 3½" x 16" strip set. Press seams toward darker fabrics. Using rotary cutter and ruler, cut eight 1½" segments from strip set.

1½

3½

Cut 8

3. Sew one unit from step 1 between two units from step 2 as shown. Press. Make four.

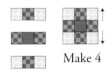

Make 4

4. Sew one 1½" x 20" Fabric D strip between two 1½" x 20" Fabric C strips to make one 3½" x 20" strip set. Press. Using rotary cutter and ruler, cut four 4½" segments from strip set.

4½

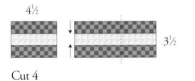

3½

Cut 4

5. Sew one unit from step 4 between two units from step 3. Press. Make two.

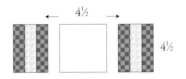

Make 2

6. Sew 4½" Fabric A square between remaining units from step 4. Press.

4½

4½

7. Sew unit from step 6 between units from step 5 as shown. Press.

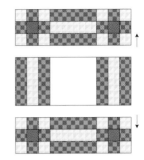

8. Sew 1" x 10½" Fabric B strips to top and bottom of block. Press seams toward border strips. Sew 1" x 11½" strips to sides. Press.

9. Trace embroidery pattern on page 95 onto Fabric A block center. Refer to Embroidery Stitch Guide on page 110. Use embroidery floss to embroider as desired.

10. Follow steps 1-3 of Layering and Finishing for the Checks and Dashes Little Wall Quilts on page 92.

MIX THE OLD
WITH THE NEW

Mixing the old with the new can be a winning combination. For a delightful decorating touch, mix your lovely new dinnerware with vintage kitchen collectibles. If you're not already a seasoned collector, kitchen goodies are an ideal place to start. The choices are abundant … pottery bowls, colorful tinware, wire utensils, vintage table linens, and the possibilities go on and on. And the best part? Many are still affordable and can be found in a variety of places such as flea markets, garage sales, and antique shops just to name a few.

Go ahead … mix it up! The surprising contrast between the precious old and the shiny new will bring your own personal look to your kitchen.

CUTTING CORNERS

1. Refer to Quick Corner Triangle directions on page 110. Sew four 3½" Fabric D squares to 6½" center square. Press.

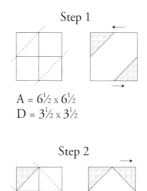

Step 1

A = 6½ x 6½
D = 3½ x 3½

Step 2

D = 3½ x 3½

2. Sew 1½" x 6½" Fabric C strips to top and bottom. Press toward strip. Then sew 1½" x 8½" Fabric C strips to sides. Press.

3. Cut 8½" Fabric B square in half twice diagonally to make four triangles.

8½
8½

4. Sew one triangle to each side of unit from step 2. Press. Carefully trim block to 10½" square. Be sure Fabric A square is centered in the block. (Trimming will cut off blue points.)

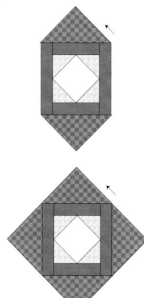

5. Refer to Quick Corner Triangle directions on page 110. Sew four 3½" Fabric C corner squares to unit from step 4. Press. Block will measure 10½" square.

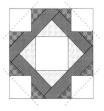

C = 3½ x 3½

6. Sew 1" x 10½" Fabric B strips to top and bottom of block. Sew 1" x 11½" strips to sides. Press seams toward border strips.

7. Trace embroidery pattern from this page onto Fabric A block center. Refer to Embroidery Stitch Guide on page 110. Use embroidery floss to embroider as desired.

8. Follow steps 1-3 of Layering and Finishing for the Checks and Dashes Little Wall Quilts on page 92.

toaster embroidery pattern for Cutting Corners

coffee pot embroidery pattern for shelf doilies

egg cup embroidery pattern for Checks and Dashes

teapot embroidery pattern for Nine Patch

BEAUTIFUL BUTTERFLIES

LOOK CLOSELY AND *you'll see them fluttering through the soft rays of summer sunshine. These beautiful butterflies invite you into a sweet-smelling garden to relax and enjoy the gorgeous blooms all around.*

What a delightful setting for a light lunch ... or just for sitting back, fluffing your pillow, and passing a lazy afternoon among fragrant flowers and delicate butterflies.

BUTTERFLY DINNERWARE

BUTTERFLY GARDEN

QUILT

Finished Size: 58" x 82"

Photo: page 96

DELICATE EMBROIDERED BUTTERFLIES HOVER *over carefully-tended "flower beds" in this colorful patchwork garden. We made this project in an assortment of our pretty pastels, but it will be lovely in any color scheme. Read all instructions before beginning and use ¼"-wide seams throughout.*

Quilt Layout

FABRIC REQUIREMENTS

Fabric A *(block centers)* - ⅞ yard light fabric

Fabric B *(corner triangles)* - Four 3½" squares each of twenty-four assorted scrappy fabrics

Fabric C *(block frames)* - One 3½" x 42" strip each of twenty-four assorted scrappy fabrics

First Accent Border - ¼ yard

Second Accent Border - ¼ yard

Border - ⅞ yard

Binding - ¾ yard

Backing - 3⅝ yards

Lightweight batting 66" x 90" piece

Embroidery floss or thread

Butterfly embroidery -

Debbie Mumm® Every Day machine embroidery card from Bernina of America, (888) BERNINA

CUTTING THE STRIPS AND PIECES

Read first paragraph of Cutting the Strips and Pieces on page 7.

Fabric A *(block centers)*

* Four 6½" x 42" strips, cut into
  * Twenty-four 6½" squares

Fabric C *(block frames)*

* Two 3½" x 12½" strips
* Two 3½" x 6½" strips

Repeat for each of twenty-four strips.

First Accent Border
* Seven 1" x 42" strips

Second Accent Border
* Seven 1" x 42" strips

Border
* Seven 4" x 42" strips

Binding
* Eight 2¾" x 42" strips

MAKING THE BLOCKS

You'll be making twenty-four framed Diamond in a Square Blocks.

Whenever possible, use the assembly line method for each step. Position pieces right sides together and line up next to your sewing machine. Stitch first unit together, then continue sewing others without breaking threads. When all units are sewn, clip threads to separate them. Press in direction of arrows in diagrams.

1. Refer to Quick Corner Triangle directions on page 110. Sew four matching 3½" Fabric B squares to each 6½" Fabric A square. Press. Make a total of twenty-four.

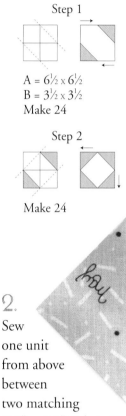

Step 1

A = 6½ x 6½
B = 3½ x 3½
Make 24

Step 2

Make 24

2. Sew one unit from above between two matching 3½" x 6½" Fabric C strips. Press. Make a total of twenty-four.

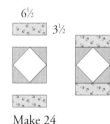

6½
3½

Make 24

3. Sew one unit from step 2 between two matching 3½" x 12½" Fabric C strips. Press. Make a total of twenty-four. Block will measure 12½".

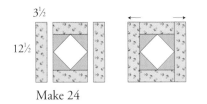

3½

12½

Make 24

4. Machine embroider butterfly pattern or trace embroidery pattern below onto Fabric A block center. Refer to Embroidery Stitch Guide on page 110. Use embroidery floss to embroider as desired.

ASSEMBLY

1. Refer to project layout on page 98. Arrange blocks in pleasing arrangement of six horizontal rows with four blocks each. Sew blocks into rows. Press seams in opposite directions from row to row.

2. Sew rows together. Press.

3. Cut one 1" x 42" first accent border strip in half and sew a half strip to two first accent border strips. Measure quilt through center from side to side. Trim strips to this measurement. Sew to top and bottom. Press toward accent border.

4. Sew remaining 1" x 42" first accent border strips together in pairs. Measure quilt through center from top to bottom. Trim strips to this measurement. Sew to sides. Press.

5. Repeat steps 3 and 4 for second accent border.

6. Measure, trim, and add 4" borders to quilt in same manner.

LAYERING AND FINISHING

1. Cut backing fabric crosswise into two equal pieces. Sew pieces together on long edges to make one 65" x 90" (approximate) backing piece. Arrange and baste backing, batting, and top together, referring to Layering the Quilt directions on page 111.

2. Hand or machine quilt as desired.

3. Cut two 2¾" x 42" binding strips in half. Sew one half to each of two 2¾" x 42" strips. Sew remaining 2¾" x 42" binding strips together in pairs and sew one remaining half to each strip. Using shorter strips for top and bottom and longer strips for sides, refer to Binding the Quilt directions on page 111 to finish.

butterfly embroidery patterns for Butterfly Garden Quilt and Flutter By Pillow

BUTTERFLY DINNERWARE

Create a perfect setting for warm sunny days with this charming melamine dinnerware adorned with delicate butterflies in shades of soft blues and yellows. For information on where to buy Debbie Mumm® dinnerware, visit www.debbiemumm.com or call (888) 819-2923.

FLUTTER BY

PILLOW

Pillow Layout

Finished Size: 16" square

Photo: page 101

❖

PAIR THIS PASTEL

PRETTY WITH

*the matching Butterfly
Garden Quilt, or place it center
stage on a sofa, rocker, or easy
chair. Read all instructions
before beginning and use
¼"-wide seams throughout.*

FABRIC REQUIREMENTS

Fabric A *(block center)* - One 6½"
square of light fabric

Fabric B *(corner triangles)* - Four 3½"
squares

Inside Border - ⅛ yard

Inside Corner Squares - Four 3"
squares

Outside Border - ⅙ yard

Outside Corner Squares - Four 3"
squares

Lining - 20" square

Batting - 20" square

Backing - ⅓ yard

Pillow form - 16" square

Embroidery floss

CUTTING THE STRIPS AND PIECES

Read first paragraph of Cutting
the Strips and Pieces on page 7.

Inside Border

❋ One 3" x 42" strip, cut into
 • Four 3" x 6½" pieces

Outside Border

❋ Two 3" x 42" strips, cut into
 • Four 3" x 11½" pieces

Backing

❋ One 11" x 42" strip, cut into
 • Two 11" x 16½" pieces

MAKING THE BLOCK

1. Refer to Quick Corner Triangle directions on page 110. Sew four 3½" Fabric B squares to opposite sides of 6½" Fabric A square. Press.

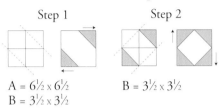

Step 1   Step 2

A = 6½ x 6½
B = 3½ x 3½   B = 3½ x 3½

2. Sew unit from above between two 3" x 6½" inside border strips. Press seams toward border strips.

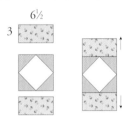

6½

3

3. Sew each remaining 3" x 6½" inside border strip between two 3" inside corner squares. Press.

6½

3

Make 2

4. Sew unit from step 2 between units from step 3. Press.

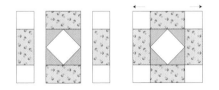

5. Sew unit from step 4 between two 3" x 11½" outside border strips. Press.

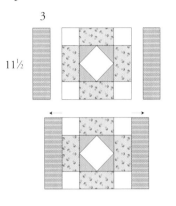

3

11½

6. Sew each remaining 3" x 11½" outside border strip between two 3" outside corner squares. Press.

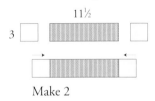

11½

3

Make 2

7. Sew unit from step 5 between units from step 6. Press.

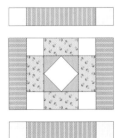

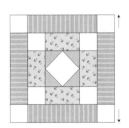

8. Machine embroider or trace embroidery pattern from page 100 onto Fabric A block center. Refer to Embroidery Stitch Guide on page 110. Use embroidery floss to embroider as desired.

9. Layer batting between top and lining. Baste. Hand or machine quilt as desired.

LAYERING AND FINISHING

1. Narrow hem one long edge of each 11" x 16½" backing piece by folding under ¼" to wrong side. Press. Fold again ¼" to wrong side. Topstitch along folded edge.

2. With right sides up, lay one backing piece over second piece so hemmed edges overlap, making single 16½" backing panel. Baste pieces together at top and bottom where they overlap. Refer to diagrams on page 38.

3. With right sides together, position and pin pillow top to backing. Using ¼" seam, sew around edges. Trim corners, turn right side out, and press.

4. Insert pillow form into pillow cover.

WELCOME BANNER

Banner Layout

Finished Size: 18" x 19½"

Photo: page 106

FAMILY AND FRIENDS WILL FEEL MORE THAN

welcome when greeted by this colorful banner in your kitchen, entry, or hall. We used nine different colors of felted wool and three different colors of embroidery floss to create the quick-fuse appliqués, but you may use as few or as many as you'd like.

FABRIC REQUIREMENTS

Background - 16" x 18" piece of felted wool

Backing - Two 18½" x 22½" panels of coordinating cotton fabric (⅔ yard)

Assorted felted wool scraps for appliqués and tabs

Notions:

- 1 yard of sewable fusible web
- Embroidery floss in assorted colors

- Dowel - ⅜" - diameter, 15" length
- Two end caps for dowel
- Acrylic paint
- Buttons - fourteen ⅜"-diameter in coordinating colors, two ¾"- diameter porcelain

[Porcelain buttons by Porcelain Rose, (562) 424-9728]

ASSEMBLING THE BACKGROUND PANEL

1. Measure down 6" from the top along the left and right sides of one 18½" x 22½" cotton panel. Mark these measurements.

2. Measure 6" across top from both left and right upper corners on same cotton panel. Mark these measurements.

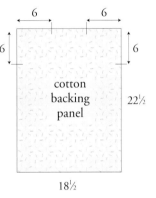

cotton backing panel
6   6
6   6
22½
18½

3. Angle a ruler across one corner, using marked measurements as a guide. Use your rotary cutter to trim corner. Repeat for other corner.

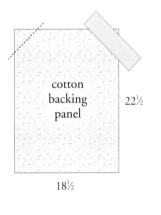

cotton backing panel
22½
18½

4. Repeat steps 1-3 to measure, mark, and trim second 18½" x 22½" cotton backing panel.

5. Position trimmed cotton backing panels right sides together. Using ¼" seam, sew around edges, leaving a 3" opening for turning. Trim corners, turn right side out, hand stitch opening closed, and press.

6. Repeat steps 1-3 to measure, mark, and trim a 3" triangle from top corners of 16" x 18" felted wool panel as shown.

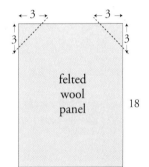

felted wool panel
3   3
3   3
18
16

QUICK-FUSE APPLIQUÉ

1. Refer to Quick-Fuse Appliqué directions on page 111. Use patterns on pages 107-108. Reverse those that are marked on pattern pieces and trace one each of pattern piece 9 and letters W, L, C, O, and M; two of letter E; and six each of pattern pieces 10 and 11 onto paper side of fusible web.

In addition, trace one regular and one reverse each of pattern pieces 1-6, 7a-h, and 8. Note: Piece 6 is the large background piece for checkerboard.

FELTED WOOL

*It's simple to give
your wool an
added richness and
fullness ... felt it!*

*The easiest way to do
this is to put it through
the wash cycle on your
washing machine
using hot water.*

*After washing, put it
into the dryer until
it is thoroughly dry.
The result will be
a thicker, fuller fabric
that will give
added texture to
your Welcome Banner.*

2. Quick-fuse butterfly layers, referring to layout on page 104 for guidance. In similar fashion, quick-fuse one small background circle to each large background circle.

3. Quick-fuse layered butterfly, layered circles, and WELCOME letters to wool panel, referring to layout on page 104 for placement.

4. Refer to Embroidery Stitch Guide on page 110. Use six strands of embroidery floss to blanket stitch around butterfly, wing checkerboard, and other appliqués as desired. Use three strands of floss to stem stitch antennae.

5. Position appliquéd wool panel face up on backing panel. Backing should extend ½" beyond bottom edge, 1" beyond side edges, and 2" beyond top edge of wool panel as shown. Refer to Embroidery Stitch Guide on page 110. Use six strands of embroidery floss to blanket stitch wool panel to backing panel.

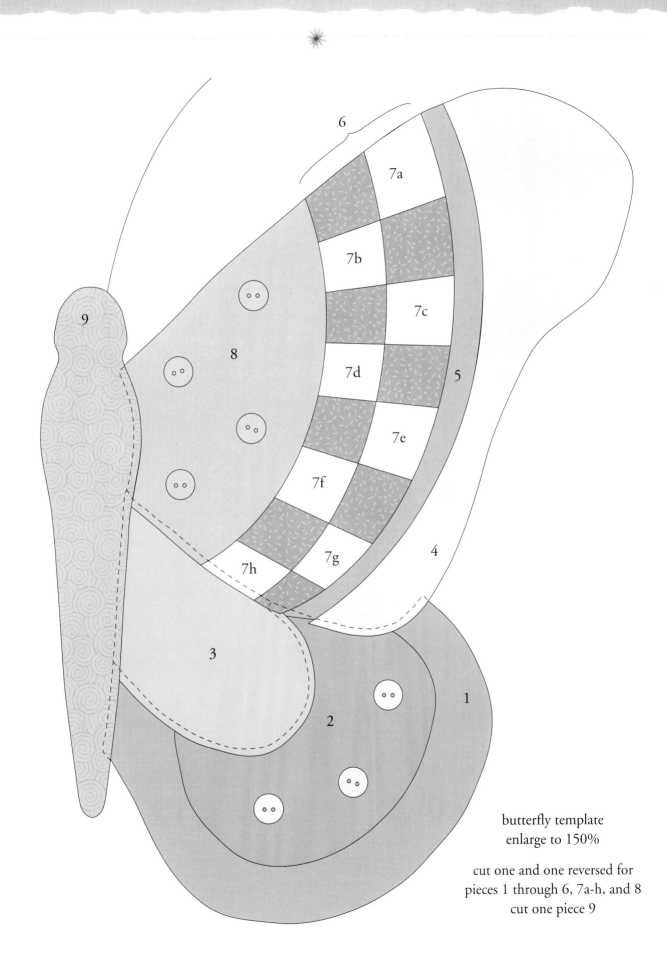

9

8

6

7a

7b

7c

7d

5

7e

7f

7g

7h

4

3

2

1

butterfly template
enlarge to 150%

cut one and one reversed for
pieces 1 through 6, 7a-h, and 8
cut one piece 9

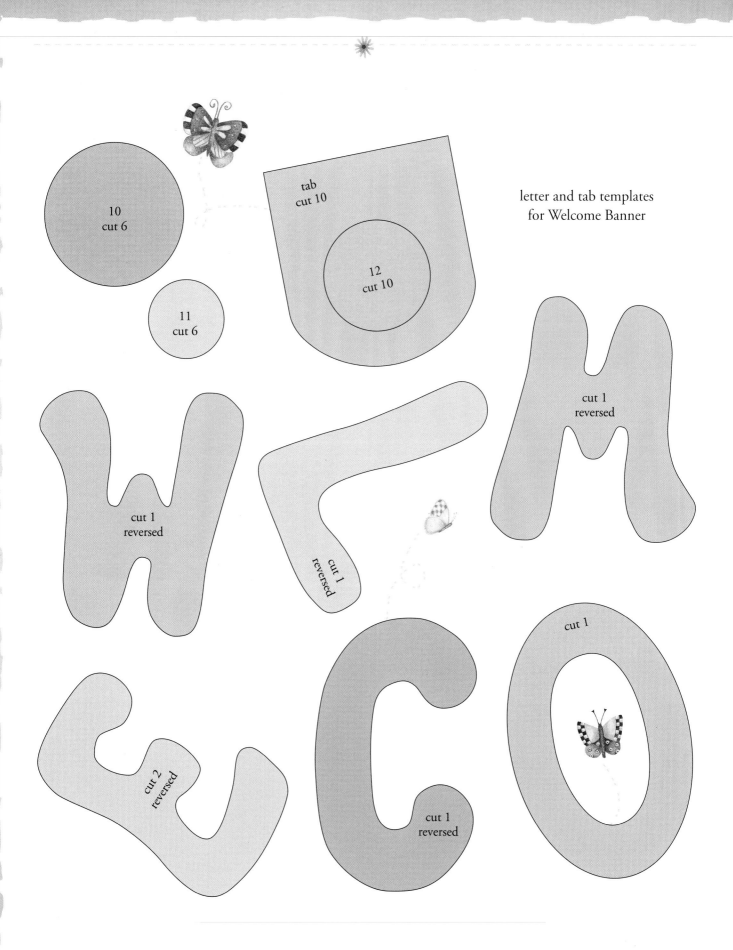

10
cut 6

11
cut 6

tab
cut 10

12
cut 10

letter and tab templates
for Welcome Banner

cut 1
reversed

cut 1
reversed

cut 1
reversed

cut 2
reversed

cut 1
reversed

cut 1

FINISHING THE BANNER

1. Use tab pattern on page 108 to make template and trace ten tabs from remaining wool scraps.

2. Turn top edge of backing to front side of wool panel.

3. Appliqué bottom edge of turned backing panel to banner front.

4. With right sides together, sew two wool tabs to top edge of backed panel as shown. Flip tabs, add two pattern piece 12 felt circles with blanket stitch, and secure with ¾"-diameter porcelain buttons, stitching through all layers of banner "sandwich."

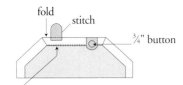

5. Refer to Quick-Fuse Appliqué directions on page 111. Trace and cut eight of pattern piece 12 onto paper side of fusible web. Quick-fuse to remaining wool tabs.

6. Whip stitch fused tabs to bottom edge of banner backing. Refer to layout on page 104 for guidance. Blanket stitch around tabs and circles.

7. Sew through all layers to attach ⅜"-diameter buttons to butterfly wings. Refer to layout on page 104 for guidance.

8. Paint dowel and dowel end caps with acrylic paint in coordinating color. Allow to dry and slip through top flap.

HAND APPLIQUÉ

Hand appliqué is easy when you start out with the right supplies. Cotton machine embroidery thread is easy to work with. Pick a color that matches the appliqué fabric as closely as possible. Use a long, thin needle like a sharp for stitching and slender appliqué or silk pins for holding shapes in place.

1. Make a plastic template for every shape in the appliqué design. Use a dotted line to show where pieces overlap.

2. Place template on right side of appliqué fabric. Trace around template.

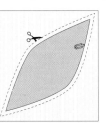

3. Cut out shapes ¼" beyond traced line.

4. Position shapes on background fabric. For pieces that overlap, follow numbers on patterns. Pieces with lower numbers go underneath; pieces with higher numbers are layered on top. Pin shapes in place.

5. Stitch shapes in order following pattern numbers. Where shapes overlap, do not turn under and stitch edges of bottom pieces. Turn and stitch the edges of the piece on top.

6. Use the traced line as your turn-under guide. Entering from the wrong side of the appliqué shape, bring the needle up on the traced line. Using the tip of the needle, turn under the fabric along the traced line. Using a blind stitch, stitch along the folded edge to join the appliqué shape to the background fabric. Turn under and stitch about ¼" at a time.

7. Clip curves and V-shapes to help the fabric turn under smoothly. Clip to within a couple threads of the traced line.

8. After stitching the entire block, place it face down on top of a thick towel and press.

QUICK CORNER TRIANGLES

Quick corner triangles are formed by simply sewing fabric squares to other squares and rectangles. The directions and diagrams with each project show you what size pieces to use and where to place square on corresponding piece. Follow steps 1–3 below to make corner triangle units.

1. With pencil and ruler, draw diagonal line on wrong side of fabric square that will form the triangle. See Diagram A. This will be your sewing line.

A.

sewing line

2. With right sides together, place square on corresponding piece. Matching raw edges, pin in place and sew ON drawn line.

B.

trim ¼" away from sewing

3. Press seam in direction of arrow as shown in step-by-step project diagram. Trim off excess fabric leaving ¼" seam allowance as shown in Diagram B. Measure completed corner triangle unit to ensure greatest accuracy.

C.

finished corner triangle unit

EMBROIDERY STITCH GUIDE

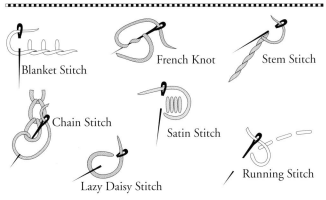

Blanket Stitch

French Knot

Stem Stitch

Chain Stitch

Satin Stitch

Lazy Daisy Stitch

Running Stitch

LAYERING THE QUILT

1. Cut backing and batting 4" to 8" larger than quilt top.

2. Lay pressed backing on bottom (right side down), batting in middle, and pressed quilt top on top. Make sure everything is centered and that backing and batting are flat. Backing and batting will extend beyond quilt top.

3. Begin basting in center and work toward outside edges. Baste vertically and horizontally, forming a 3" – 4" grid. Baste or pin completely around edge of quilt top. Quilt as desired.

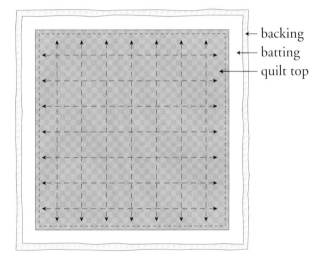

← backing
← batting
← quilt top

BINDING THE QUILT

1. Trim batting and backing to ¼" from raw edge of quilt top.

2. Fold and press binding strips in half lengthwise with wrong sides together.

3. With raw edges even, lay binding strips on top and bottom edges of quilt top. Sew through all layers, ¼" from quilt edge. Press binding away from quilt top. Trim excess length of binding.

4. Sew remaining two binding strips to quilt sides. Press and trim excess length.

5. Folding top and bottom first, fold binding around to back. Press and pin in position. Hand stitch binding in place.

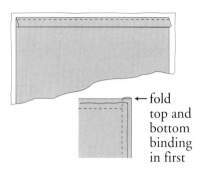

← fold top and bottom binding in first

QUICK-FUSE APPLIQUÉ

Quick-fuse appliqué is a method of adhering appliqué pieces to a background with fusible web. For quick and easy results, simply quick-fuse appliqué pieces in place. Use sewable, lightweight fusible web, for the projects in this book. Finishing raw edges with stitching is desirable. Laundering is not recommended unless edges are finished.

1. With paper side up, lay fusible web over appliqué design. Leaving ½" space between pieces, trace all elements of design. Cut around traced pieces, approximately ¼" outside traced line. See Diagram A.

A.
fusible web

2. With paper side up, position and iron fusible web to wrong side of selected fabrics. Follow manufacturer's directions for iron temperature and fusing time. Cut out each piece on traced line. See Diagram B.

B.
fabric-wrong side

3. Remove paper backing from pieces. A thin film will remain on wrong side. Position and fuse all pieces of one appliqué design at a time onto background, referring to color photos for placement.

DISCOVER MORE FROM DEBBIE MUMM®

Here's a sampling of the many other quilting and home décor books by Debbie Mumm®. These books are available at your local quilt shop, by calling (888) 819-2923, or by shopping online at www.debbiemumm.com.

Debbie Mumm's®
Floral Inspirations
80-page, soft cover
Suggested Retail Price $19.95
Plus shipping and handling

Debbie Mumm's®
Birdhouses for Every Season
112-page, soft cover
Suggested Retail Price $27.95
Plus shipping and handling

Woodland Christmas
80-page, soft cover
Suggested Retail Price $23.95
Plus shipping and handling

Decorator Teapot Set!

BUY TWO, GET ONE FREE!

The stylized beauty of garden flowers and a sophisticated pastel palette of sage and lavender come together in this delightful collection of mini teapots by Debbie Mumm®. For a limited time only, buy two teapots and get the third one free! Mini teapots should be hand-washed and are not for use in a microwave oven. Offer is good through 12/31/02 or while supplies last. Regular Price $29.85, **Special Offer $19.90** plus shipping and handling. Order now by calling **(888) 819-2923**.

SKU#81050

Enhance your home with Debbie Mumm®

www.debbiemumm.com

Our website, **www.debbiemumm.com** is loaded with great information and free projects to make your home comfortable and inviting. Feature articles on home decorating, cooking, gardening, and holidays are sure to inspire your creativity. Our Projects of the Month offer step-by-step instructions on charming quilting and craft projects to add handmade warmth and beauty to every room. More than 200 products are also available on our website to make purchasing Debbie Mumm® products easy and convenient. Visit **www.debbiemumm.com** regularly for the latest seasonal ideas and products.

CREDITS

Designed by Debbie Mumm®

Special thanks to my creative teams:

EDITORIAL/PROJECT DESIGN

Pamela Mostek: Publications Manager

Laura Reinstatler: Editor

Darra Williamson: Writer

Carolyn Lowe: Quilt and Craft Designer

Susan Nelsen: Quilt and Craft Designer

Jean Van Bockel: Quilt and Craft Designer

Jackie Saling: Craft Designer

Candy Huddleston: Seamstress

Nona King: Machine Quilter

Wanda Jeffries: Machine Quilter

BOOK DESIGN & PRODUCTION

Mya Brooks: Production Director

Marcia Smith: Art Director

Tom Harlow: Graphics Manager

Heather Hughes: Graphic Designer

J. Craig Sweat Photography

Barros & Barros Photography
Beautiful Butterflies

ART TEAM

Lou McKee, Sr. Artist

Kathy Arbuckle

Sandy Ayars

Heather Butler

Gil-Jin Foster

Kathy Riedinger

Revised ©2001 Debbie Mumm, Inc.
Printed in China

Source Code:
401-01003

COUNTRY SETTINGS